What

"Jeff nails the psyche of a woman and gives page-by-page cheat sheets on how to speak our language. This book will turn *any* marriage around!" –**VERONICA DEL ROSARIO**, CEO of Pump Up Cinema

"Jeff has a mighty gift. A few chapters in, I knew my marriage and I were gonna have words. I have an awesome relationship with my wife and love her deeply, but this book called me to a much higher plane. Guys, this is the marriage you've always wanted to have. This is the husband you've always wanted to *be*. Go for it!" –**AUSTIN PECK**, Actor, *Days of Our Lives*

"After two decades of clinical work and over 30,000 hours of experience, I found this book a breath of fresh air. Raw, honest, and well-written, I consider it the owner's manual for reconnecting with your partner. Read it, dig deep, and read it again. Whether your relationship is a distant or dynamic one, this book offers a massive upgrade." –**DR. WILLIAM LIBRIZZI, PsyD, LPC, ACS**; Associate Professor, The Graduate School of Psychology, Charleston Southern University; Director of The Wellspring Center

"What a gem! Filled with *rare* insight. This book needs to be in the hands of every married couple! To every man frustrated in his marriage, please read. To every woman frustrated in her marriage, please read." –**KELLY MASTER**, Director of For Dignity

"A must-read for every guy who's ready to put an end to the bad habits that have crept into his most important relationship. As one who's passionate about building strong and sexy marriages, I highly recommend this exceptional little book! I've put some of its simple strategies to good use and seen the impact it's had on my wife and marriage. Grab it today and become irresistible again!" –**TONY DILORENZO**, Founder of ONEExtraordinaryMarriage.com; Co-Host of the #1 Marriage Podcast on iTunes

Published in the United States by Your Turn Media

ISBN 978-0-9976-5611-4

Cover design by Natascha Helbing

Contact the author:
wifemagnet.me
facebook.com/wifemagnet

To Jack

I couldn't be prouder of you and the young man you're growing up to be. I'm so glad I get to be your dad.

To His Mom

The truths you taught me, though I learned them too late, are helping men and marriages around the world. Thank you.

Acknowledgments

Dr. Wil Librizzi (The Wellspring Center): This book started in your office. Thank you for helping me go deep.

Patrice Perrone: My journal entry from a year ago contains your admonishment, "Write! Get to it! Chop-chop!" I listened.

Devin + Shirley Burke, Chris + Jessica Francis: This book would still be a PDF without your help. Thank you for believing in me.

Veronica del Rosario: You cheered me on the loudest and longest!

Shane Trowbridge: Your early criticisms made me change course and write a better book.

Kevin Borkoski: Your well-thought-out suggestions saved it from certain doom.

Mom: Your obsession with *Taken* inspired my favorite chapter.

Jonathan Mellett: The drawings are perfect! Your check is in the mail.

Emily Mellett: I didn't want to hear it at first, but dagnabbit, you were right — fewer cuss words make the book more accessible.

Kenny Champion, Sherri Kovan: My two linchpins. Your small tweaks and painstaking edits were the finishing touches I couldn't find anywhere else.

Armando Trejo: You were my wing man down the stretch.

Hal Elrod, John Lee Dumas, Michael Hyatt, Steven Pressfield, Seth Godin: You taught me how to ignore the small voices and take my turn. *Thank you.*

Chandler Bolt, Tom Corson-Knowles, Steve Scott, Dave Chesson, Donald Miller: I would have been lost without the trail you set.

Gary Cooper, Jeffery David, Elizabeth Neary, Chuck Morelli, Carl Thomas, David Wygal, Linda Schreiber, David Hauschild, Jim Berge, Philip Wagner, John Crowley, Meredith Koloski, Chris McNeil, Alex Jones-Moreno, Joe Brown, Lisa Poulos, Jason Brandt, Anthony Morici: Your input and encouragement kept this husky mushing.

Everyone who read my Advance Review Copy in exchange for an honest review: Thank you for propelling me toward my goal of transforming men and marriages around the world. You're a part of each miracle.

This isn't my book, it's *ours*. I hope you like it!

Contents

Have Cone, Will Travel

I closed my eyes and she slipped away.[1]
–TOM SCHOLZ

Have you ever seen a "conehead" in your neighborhood? Not the *Beldar* kind made famous by Dan Aykroyd, but the canine kind, the four-legged variety. I saw one on my block yesterday. A tan, scruffy, medium-sized mutt walking alongside its owner. Poor dog. Most likely healing from a wound, its head was completely ensconced in a plastic cone.

That was me, only the two-legged variety.

I can't pinpoint precisely when, but a few years into my marriage, I started wearing a cone around my neck. My field of vision was limited to one thing: getting ahead at work. I excelled there. I was respected there. I was applauded there. That's the problem with cones when they fit just right — we forget they're temporary and get used to them. Mine stayed on for an entire decade.

Around the 12-year mark of our marriage, my wife decided she was tired of not being noticed. Tired of trying to fit inside my cone. She left me and found someone who saw what I had stopped seeing years ago — her beauty, passion, charm, and worth. Apparently, her new boyfriend doesn't know the first thing about wearing a cone.

PAIN TRAIN, NOW BOARDING

My wife didn't leave all at once, but in stages. She pulled away emotionally, then sexually, before leaving for good. If you're like the majority of men either married or in a committed relationship, you picked up this book because your sex life has been somewhat less than stellar recently. In fact, your intimacy timeline might look something like this:

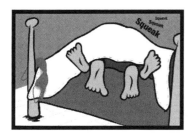 

Ouch! I remember those days vividly. They sucked for a number of reasons:

1. The woman I married is smokin' hot.

2. I saw her in various stages of undress throughout the week.

3. Everyone on TV is having lots of great sex.

4. Everyone I know is having lots of great sex (so I thought).

5. Rejection is hard enough in the real world; in marriage it's devastating.

We've all faced our fair share of rejection. As a kid, I was bullied and called "dumb Polock" for having the wrong last name. My own father told me I was a loser who would never amount to anything. But whatever form rejection took throughout my life, it paled in comparison to what I experienced in a sexless marriage. I know what it's like to have your wife get up and walk out of the room when you walk in. To refuse to make eye contact. To recoil from your touch. One scene that played out quite frequently in our home was me walking into our bedroom just as my naked, glistening, fresh-out-of-the-shower wife frantically grabbed a towel to cover herself and hide her beauty and sexuality from me. The message was clear: "That's as close as you're gonna get."

I understand your frustration. I understand your anger. *I understand your pain.*

I can help.

This book is my story. I didn't write it to put *author* after my name. I wrote it to help you get your mojo back. To help you identify the things that have shipwrecked your sex life. To help you avoid the mistakes I made. And, in case it's heading in that direction, to save you from the devastation, emotional trauma, and financial bloodletting known as divorce.

You won't find any parlor tricks inside, no decoys or sleight-of-hand maneuvers designed to lure your wife back into the sack. Instead, it's crammed with practical ways to become the kind of husband she'll respect, admire, and *want* to wrap her legs around.

In all honesty, this isn't a book. It's boot camp. I'm not here to baby you. And no, I'm not here to make you feel stupid. I'm here to call out the best in you! It's the reason I leap out of bed every morning.

THE EVIDENCE IS IN

What you're about to learn is revolutionary. For the past few years, I've taught these proven principles to the guys I coach. The transformation we've witnessed has been nothing short of miraculous — think "night and day."

I have a bold claim to make: No matter how bad things are right now, you're only one or two *Aha!* moments away from having steamy sex with your wife again.

I couldn't be more serious.

Prepare to see her light up again when you enter the room. Prepare to be greeted with a long, awkward-for-everyone-else kiss. Prepare to feel her hand reach for yours. Prepare to have *her* initiate sex. Prepare for a marriage beyond your wildest dreams!

It's your turn.

"My Wife Gave Me This Dumb Book"

*The sooner you step away from your comfort zone,
the sooner you'll realize it wasn't really all that comfortable.*
−EDDIE HARRIS JR.

If your wife gave you this book, you're incredibly fortunate. It means she wants more from your relationship. It means she wants to be closer to you. It means *she* wants to have great sex again. You're practically rounding third.

Don't rule out the possibility it's a cry for help. Giving you this book could be her way of saying, "I'm sad about us. Some days I feel like giving up. I don't know how to get your attention anymore."

Maybe you found this book in your briefcase. Or on the kitchen counter next to your keys. Maybe a threatening sticky note graced the cover. Regardless of whence it came, please don't miss the powerful underlying message: in spite of all that's transpired, your wife is still holding out hope you could be an intimate, loving couple again.

That's huge.

When women lose hope in a relationship, they begin devising an exit strategy. As bad as things are today, they could get much worse. I know from experience divorce is spelled P-A-I-N. The pain of loss. The pain of regret. The pain of *"If only."* In some cases, the pain of betrayal and infidelity. It's the reason we scoff at Hollywood press releases when newly-divorced celebrity couples say, "We still love each other. We'll always be close friends." C'mon. Like we're that stupid.

Don't let appearances fool you. This is *much more* than a book. It's an invitation from your better half. To start over. To move past your past. To reclaim the magic. To build something breathtaking.

Three cheers for your wife!

Before We Begin

*We cannot solve our problems with the same thinking
we used when we created them.*

−ALBERT EINSTEIN

You're not a failure.

You just need a new strategy.

Because the one that's currently in place — you wait for her to change, she waits for you to change — ain't workin'. Never has, actually. Not in any marriage. The only thing that *does* work is when one spouse is willing to break the cycle and do what's never been done before.

That's you.

YOUR LATENT SUPERPOWER

I don't have a magic wand. If I did, I'd wave it and you'd be moments away from "doing it like they do on the Discovery Channel."[2] Fortunately, you don't need me *or* a magic wand. You have something far more powerful in your possession: the power of choice.

"That's it?!"

That's everything.

I'll never forget my Red-Sea-parting moment. At the time, I was a scornful, stewing, finger-pointing mess. My wife had just filed for divorce and my brain was stuck in a rut called *"How could she?!"* A trusted friend interrupted my pity party with this pointed question:

"Jeff, what do you *want?"*

My heart burst. I knew immediately what I wanted — I wanted her back! I wanted to hold her in my arms. I wanted to stare into those beautiful brown eyes. I wanted her to be happy again. In that pivotal moment, I knew all that mattered was us. I wanted *us* back.

The clouds lifted. The resentment faded. Weakness took a back seat to strength that day. I became a man on a mission. Not simply to win her back, but to become the kind of man she could love and trust again. I chose to accept full responsibility for everything I had done (or hadn't done) that contributed to the mess our marriage was in. I'm not exaggerating when I say my entire life began to change with that one decision. A few months later I read this quote by Hal Elrod, author of *The Miracle Morning,* confirming the path I had embarked upon:

"The moment you take responsibility for *everything* in your life, is the moment you can change *anything* in your life."

As long as I pointed at my wife and fixated on *her* shortcomings, I stayed stuck. But once I decided to take honest inventory of myself — acknowledging my offenses, refusing to blame-shift when faced with my failures as a husband — an unstoppable force was unleashed. A force that continues to bring radical improvement to every aspect of my life.

WITHHOLDING SEX & OTHER CRIMES AGAINST HUMANITY

What I'm about to say will sound like we're letting your wife off the hook. Far from it! Downsizing your sex life is a unilateral decision she had no business making. I read your wedding vows: "For richer or for poorer" made the list; "In sickness and in health" was there; but "Whether we have sex or not" was nowhere to be found. I'm guessing you wouldn't have stepped foot on that altar or stood underneath that wedding arch if it was. Hell, I would have stopped the ceremony myself and I barely know you:

> "Ahem … excuse me … I don't know the couple very well, I'm just here as someone's date, but this marriage won't work, not without lots of sex. There's no way I can sit here and support this decision. I'll just grab some shrimp on my way out. Thank you."

So no, I'm not absolving your wife of blame. She brought her own colorful assortment of baggage into your marriage, and most likely you only saw the smaller carry-on pieces prior to takeoff. *Of course* she plays a part in all of this!

But I don't have her ear, I have yours.

THE ROAD LESS TRAVELED

OK, this will only sting for a moment. It's not something you'll overhear in locker rooms or gentlemen's clubs or anywhere else sheep congregate. It's reserved for boot camps and books like this one — whose goal is turning ordinary men into Spartan warriors. Bite into this sobering but empowering truth:

You brought your marriage to where it is today.

On purpose? I seriously doubt it. "Drift apart and stop having sex" certainly wasn't high on my list of marital aspirations.

It was, however, a painful reality. One that emerged on my watch.

Look at that sentence again. Wrestle with it if you need to. Kick and scream if you need to. I'm not going anywhere.

You brought your marriage to where it is today.

You.

You led it here. You've got to own that, no matter how unfair it sounds. Because if that's true, so is this:

You can bring it somewhere else.

When you come to grips with the idea that your leadership (or lack thereof) brought your marriage to the pitiful place it is today, you're immediately empowered to lead it to a much better place.

Peter Parker's uncle Ben was right: "With great power comes great responsibility."[3] Yet the inverse is equally true: "With great responsibility comes great power." If you brought your marriage *here,* you also have the ability to bring it *somewhere else.*

You.

THING ONE & THING TWO

Getting unstuck and bringing sexy back won't happen in a vacuum. It will require two things: humility and courage. Both are essential. Both are precursors to all lasting change. Together they're the high-octane fuel for breakthrough and success.

Humility is not weakness. It's *strength.* It's having the stones to say, "My current approach isn't working. I'm tired of banging my head against the same wall. There's too much at stake — my dignity, my marriage, the kind of home my kids grow up in. I'm ready to chart a new course!"

Courage is humility's fraternal twin. It's having the guts to say, "Regardless of who's right or wrong, I'm taking full responsibility for my contribution to the sorry state of our marriage. No more finger-pointing. No more excuses. I'm not looking for a quick fix. I'm ready to go the distance. I'm ready to do whatever it takes to regain my wife's respect and build a world-class marriage!"

If you mean it, turn the page.

It's time to break the cycle and do what you've never done before.

Women Are Liars

When a woman is silent, listen to her very carefully.
—LILKA

Women are liars. Every last one. You need to know that. Most would rather eat their young than tell their husbands the truth.

This snapshot from my own marriage might sound eerily familiar:

> **Me:** "Hey babe, you seem quiet. Is anything wrong?"
>
> **My Lying Wife:** "No."
>
> **Me:** "Are you sure?"
>
> **My Lying Wife:** "Yeah."
>
> **Me:** "C'mon, what's bothering you?"
>
> **My Lying Wife:** "Nothing."
>
> **Me:** "OK, I'm gonna head to the gym and get a workout."
>
> **My Lying Wife:** "Fine."

All lies.

Spoken to a clueless husband who bowed out too soon.

These "conversations" typically ended with me shrugging my shoulders and muttering a semi self-congratulatory, "I tried," as I walked out the door.

That was the biggest lie of the day.

I hadn't tried at all.

I had things to do, and I knew (on a subconscious level, at least) helping my wife get unstuck could take a while. A half-hearted attempt is all I had time for. So I chose to ignore her tone of voice and glaring body language. I chose to stick with *my* agenda rather than connect with her in a meaningful way.

I chose *me* over her.

In doing so, I unwittingly sent one of the most hurtful messages a man could ever send his wife:

"I don't care about your pain."

I'll never forget the day I awoke to this realization. It was too late — my wife was gone — but it hit me like a thousand blunt knives. The opportunities I had missed! To be there for her when she needed me most. To look deeply into her eyes and say, "My husband radar tells me something's bothering you. I have a lot to do today, but it can all take a number and wait. Nothing is more important to me than *you*. I won't try to fix anything…but tell me about your day. I want to hear what happened. I want to share this load with you."

Moments of pure relationship gold — squandered.

Clueless has a price.

MIND READERS NEED NOT APPLY

Instead, as I walked out the door, my wife was left feeling even more unloved and alone. And whatever *was* bothering her — the thing she desperately needed to talk about — continued to fester like an infected wound.

On many occasions, by the time I meandered home, that wound had metastasized and grown to dreadful proportions.

> **My Wife:** "You don't care about me! All you care about is yourself! You have no idea what happened to me today, no idea why I've been sad all afternoon. And do you care?! *No!*
>
> [mocking tone begins]
>
> " 'I'm going to the gym. I'm going to work on my-*self*. I'm going to take care of my-*self*.'
>
> [mocking tone ends]
>
> "Fine! While you're at it, you can make dinner for yourself, too! I'll reach out to someone else. I have plenty of friends who actually *care* about me."

It's likely you've been on the receiving end of something similar. Deserved maybe, but in the moment, it feels like a low blow. Time to defend myself. Time to pull out my illusory ace in the hole:

Me: "That's not fair! I *asked* you this morning if anything was wrong, and you said 'No.' How am I supposed to know what's bothering you?! I'm not a mind reader!"

WIN-NING!

Right?

Hardly. How dumb was I? As if my wife would respond, "Wait … you're not a mind reader?! Oh honey, thank you for being so honest. Just think, for *years* I've been under the impression you could read minds. That's why I didn't tell you what was wrong this morning. I kept thinking, 'Why doesn't he just read my mind like he always does?' I'm so sorry. You're right, it was unfair of me to lash out at you the way I did. Please forgive me for being such a brat. Phew, I'm glad we cleared that up. Why don't you take a shower, and we'll make love in front of the fireplace."

Didn't happen.

Mind reading, if there were such a thing, wouldn't help my cause or yours. Here's the simple reason why:

She doesn't want you to read her mind.

That would be too easy. That would allow you to stay on the surface. She's a treasure trove of beauty and complexity. She wants you to *dig*. She wants you to break a sweat. She wants you to work for it. She wants you to pull it out of her. She wants to know she's your priority.

She wants to know you care about her pain.

Reasonable expectations, for sure. After all, you did marry her. You did pursue her with flair and passion. Why wouldn't you now? Well, you would ... unless something has changed. Unless your feelings for her have changed. Unless your love for her isn't what it used to be.

Unless *she's* not what she used to be.

Yup, that's where her mind goes. She's not upset because you couldn't read her mind. She's upset because you gave up so easily and what that must mean.

THE PROBLEM WITH THE PROPOSAL

Let me show you where the problem began.

Go back a few years to the moment you got down on one knee, pulled out a small velvety case, opened the snapping-action lid, presented her with a sparkly token of your love, smiled wide, and popped the question: "Will you marry me?"

The majority of men don't arrive here casually. This is a big decision. The biggest. In fact, we've put so much thought into choosing our life's partner, that by the time we *do* pop the question, feelings are pushed to the side because it's "Go" time! Regardless of the actual words we use, what we're essentially saying when we propose is:

"I like everything I've seen so far. Will you marry me?"

No problem there.

The problem is she heard something *much* different. She heard:

> "I like everything I've seen so far, but realize I've only scratched the surface of who you are. I want to spend the rest of my life unearthing your hidden treasures. Will you marry me? Will you let me be the one who goes deep with you? Deeper than anyone else has ever gone?"

Big difference.

In the same way you long to explore every curve and contour of her body, your wife longs for you to explore every nuance and complexity of her soul. Her true self. Her essence. The parts that won't wrinkle with age. Her longings. Her loves. Her fears. Her deepest hurts. What angers her. What makes her tick. What she dreams about. The goals she would set if she knew you wouldn't laugh.

Loving a woman is a journey of discovery. If you're not willing to go deep with her, you had no business marrying her.

> "The biggest coward is a man who awakens a woman's love with no intention of loving her." (Bob Marley)

So the next time she's quiet and mopey, and a black cloud hangs over your home, remember:

She doesn't want a mind reader.

She wants her husband to leave the shallows and go deep with her.

Better Sex Guarantee #1
-Anticipate Her Needs-

When I consider what tremendous consequences come from little things,
I am tempted to think there are no little things.
—BRUCE BARTON

James Bond taught us two very important things about the opposite sex:

1. Despite what political correctness propagates, most women, no matter how strong and capable they are, still enjoy being plucked from danger by a rugged and well-dressed man.

2. They're also eager to take their clothes off for the guy who saves the day.

While the overwhelming majority of us will never be called upon to rescue our wives from international crime syndicates or runaway trains, opportunities to be their heroes present themselves on a regular basis. Sadly, to the untrained eye, these golden opportunities often go unrecognized. They're passed over as "too small to make a difference." Nothing could be further from the truth.

Little things make *all* the difference.

A panicked phone call one afternoon from my angry and exasperated wife drove this point home. We had recently moved from California to New Jersey, and she wasn't familiar with the lay of the land. When you add nasty weather, bone-jarring potholes, poor signage, circles, roundabouts, toll booths, impatient drivers, rude drivers, belligerent drivers, rapid lane merges, never-ending road work, industrial stench, and rush hour traffic rivaling that of Los Angeles — you'll understand why driving the northeast corridor isn't one of her favorite pastimes.

On this particular stormy afternoon she was driving to JFK International Airport in Queens — en route to visit her sick father in Utah — when all hell broke loose. A multi-cell cluster of thunderstorms assaulted the area with the speed and fury of a blitzkrieg invasion. Heavy rain, high winds, and hail pelted her car. She couldn't see five feet in front of her. To make matters worse, she was low on fuel and had missed her exit. Now she was lost and would probably miss her flight. That's when she pulled over and called her would-be hero.

Guess what I got blamed for?

All of it.

The harsh weather. The empty tank. The wrong turn. The missed flight. The ruined trip.

In her defense, I was guilty as charged. I *knew* she didn't like driving to the airport alone. I *knew* she was anxious about the massive storms threatening the coast. I *knew* she was sketchy on how to program her GPS. I *knew* her morning had been hectic. I *knew* she hadn't gassed up before hitting the road.

It was my perfectly-scripted 007 opportunity.

One I failed to show up for.

Imagine if I had. Imagine the difference a little thoughtfulness would have made that day. Imagine if I had changed my plans and driven her to the airport instead. Imagine if I had dropped her off at the curb with a kiss — delivering my precious cargo to JetBlue in one piece — safe, dry, calm, and collected. At the very least, I could have filled her tank and programmed her GPS that morning, or arranged for a friend to chauffeur her to JFK.

Imagine how completely different that phone call would have sounded:

> "Hi honey, I'm at the gate. We haven't even boarded yet, and I'm missing you already! You made me feel sooooo special today. You really know how to make my heart thump. Thanks for making sure my trip got off to such a good start! I'll call you when I land. *Mmmwah!*"

Imagine our reunion a few nights later. I'm betting she would have worn something from her *For Your Eyes Only* drawer.

LITTLE IS THE NEW BIG

Saving the day comes in small packages. We're remiss to accept this fact because it flies in the face of popular culture. We're trained from an early age to dismiss the small while placing an inordinate amount of value on *the big*. the dazzling! the wow! the grand slam! the jackpot! the oscar winner! the richest! the sexiest! the brightest! the best!

Yet intimate and lasting marriages are forged when we learn to think small — that is, anticipate the day-to-day needs of our wives and spring into action *before* we're asked.

That's worth repeating.

Intimate and lasting marriages are forged when we anticipate the day-to-day needs of our wives and spring into action *before* we're asked.

If my wife has to *ask* me to help carry in groceries from her car, I automatically rank lower on the "shows-that-he-cares" scale than the store clerk who offered to load those same bags into her car just a few minutes prior.

> **Store Clerk:** "Can I help you with those bags, ma'am? They look heavy."
>
> **My Wife:** "That's very nice of you to offer. Thank you."
>
> **Store Clerk:** "Happy to help."

It's the stuff workplace affairs are made of.

I'm not implying women are shallow or easily beguiled. A happily married woman typically doesn't get swept off her feet by a prowling co-worker. But if her husband's head is in the sand, chances are high she'll wind up in bed with someone else. Someone who anticipates her needs and consistently does the little things that brighten her day. Even if that someone is unkempt, overweight, and not much of a head turner.

> **Her Co-Worker:** "Here's the report you printed. I saw it in the copy room."
>
> **Your Wife:** "I was just about to get up and go get it. Thank you!"

> **Her Co-Worker:** "You look tired."
>
> **Your Wife:** "Ughh, I hardly slept. My youngest was up coughing all night."
>
> **Her Co-Worker:** "Go home and get some rest. I'll finish the proposal we're working on."
>
> **Your Wife:** "You're the best. I owe you."

> **Her Co-Worker:** "You like your coffee black, right? I grabbed this for you on the way in."
>
> **Your Wife:** "You read my mind! That's so thoughtful of you."

Hardly spectacular.

Just little things, done consistently over time, that lead to exponential gains. Darren Hardy coined it "the compound effect"[4] in his best-selling book of the same name. My favorite illustration of the compound effect and its extraordinary power begins with a simple question, "Which would you rather have: one million dollars cash today — right now — or a single penny doubled every day for a month?" Most of us wouldn't think twice about it. Give me the million, baby! We're eating filet tonight!

Just for fun, though, let's select the penny. My son and I did this recently using the wall calendar that hangs in our kitchen. We chose a month with 31 days and tracked our little penny's progress by recording its growing value each day.

- On the first day of the month, we wrote *1¢*.

- On day two, our penny doubles, so we wrote *2¢*. Hardly spectacular, but let's keep going.

- On day seven we clock in at a whopping 64 cents. Not even a dollar yet.

- At the end of two weeks — with nearly half the month gone — our total cash in hand is just $81.92. So far, this feels like a big mistake.

- A week later — on day 21 — we've rallied and reached $10,485.76. Impressive, but paltry compared to the million we left on the table.

- But hang in there. Because four weeks after our experiment began — on day 28 — our little, insignificant, looked-down-upon penny has mushroomed in value to $1,342,177.28.

- At month's end — day 31 — we're awash in dead presidents. To the tune of $10,737,418.24.

Filet for everyone!

Men with blistering hot sex lives understand the compound effect — the power of little things, done consistently over time, that lead to exponential gains.

Those of us on divorce row don't.

THE TROUBLE WITH EASY

The compound effect is *already* at work in your marriage. It's either working for you or against you.[5] Constantly. It's at work as you read these words. You can't stop it. You can only reap its rewards…or suffer its consequences.

By your actions:

- You're either building up your bride — or slowly tearing her down.

- You're either filling her tank — or slowly draining it dry.

- You're either moving toward your wife — or gradually drifting away from her.

- You're either increasing the likelihood of mind-blowing sex — or reducing it ever-so-slightly with each missed opportunity to serve her and be her hero.

There's no middle ground.

Then why don't more of us put the compound effect to work in our favor? Why do we carelessly gamble away the admiration and respect of our wives? Why do we jeopardize our chances of having a happy and sexually-satisfying marriage?

Here's why: The small, simple actions we take — the ones that add up over time and make us irresistible to the women we love — are easy to do, but they're also easy *not* to do.[6] Because if we don't do them, our marriages won't suffer.

At least, not today.

Let's put this dynamic in a different context for a moment. I think it will help. Let's suppose you recently made a commitment to lose 20 pounds and get fit. Sneaking a glazed donut in the break room won't add inches to your waistline. At least, not today. Sleeping in and skipping your spin class on Saturday morning won't have a noticeable negative impact on your overall health. At least, not today. Hitting the McDonald's drive-thru on your way home from work won't make you sick or end your life prematurely. At least, not today. But over time it will. You can count on it. Just ask Morgan Spurlock.

OK, bring it back to the bedroom.

I've only been married once, but I've heard that women of all stripes enjoy having their backs scratched before bed. Makes them purr like a kitten. My wife was one of them. A brief back scratch after turning out the lights helped her unwind and fall asleep. For the sake of this example, let's assume your wife is wired the same way. If you *don't* scratch her back this evening, will she rush to the courthouse tomorrow and file for divorce? Probably not. If you *do* scratch her back this evening, will your marital bond be radically restored overnight? Probably not. But don't underestimate the staggering power of the compound effect. A two-minute back scratch, done consecutively over many nights, grows exponentially just like our little penny. Get started and before you know it, your sex life will be doing handsprings.

You can count on it.

If you don't believe me, try it for 31 days. Two minutes every night. Offer before she can ask. Just two minutes. Not a second more. It's easy to do.

It's also easy not to do.

There's the rub. Putting off what you *could* do today to bless your wife and affirm your commitment to her — even if it feels insignificant in the moment — will cost you. Delaying our penny experiment just one week would have cost us over 10 million dollars by month's end!

The compound effect never takes a day off. It's always at work.

Either for you or against you.

GAINED IN TRANSLATION

It took some time, but my desirability ratings eventually surpassed those of every grocery store bagger in Los Angeles. Once I ascertained my wife didn't actually enjoy lugging 30-pound bags (whose handles tore off) from her car to the kitchen, I sprang into action and seized the opportunity to be her hero. Gallanting to the driveway to unload her SUV only took a few minutes, and only required an ounce of effort, but made a palpable difference in our home. The kind of difference that can snowball into really good sex.

Due to my wife's unique wiring, unloading the car after her weekly trip to the grocery store was the relational equivalent of foreplay. I seriously doubt she ever heard me say, "I'll bring the bags in, honey." Those words never reached her ears. They were drowned out by the running commentary of the little person in her head who, unbeknownst to me, translated my actions in real time. Instead, my wife heard:

- "You're my priority."

- "I care about how your day is going."

- "I'm grateful for all you do."

- "Thank you for making our house a home."

- "I will always use my strength to serve you."

Thank you, little person!

Women are verbal creatures, remember. It's the message that counts. It's what she hears in her head that counts. It's what the little person says that counts. Not how trivial *we* think our actions are.

I realize it's presumptuous, but I'm proposing a minor revision of the timeless idiom, "Actions speak louder than words."

Actions *are* the louder words.

THE SPY WHO LOVED ME

During the first few years of our marriage, I discovered a handful of little things that had a disproportionate impact on our wedded bliss. Sadly, I grossly underestimated their importance. It's part of the reason my wife vacated our home, emotionally and sexually, before leaving for good.

Rather than simply list them as action items, I'm going to play medium for a moment and summon my wife onto the page. Pretend she's the one about to speak:

- "Jeff, when you organize our digital photos every month, I get to enjoy them and share them with my family. That makes me happy." (i.e., "That turns me on.")

- "When we have a dinner party, and you're dressed and ready to welcome guests as they arrive, it allows me to focus on the meal I'm preparing. That puts me at ease." (i.e., "That turns me on.")

- "When you maintain a life insurance policy, I know the kids and I will be OK if something terrible were to happen. That makes me feel secure." (i.e., "That turns me on.")

- "When you pay our bills on time, I worry less and sleep better at night. That turns me on." (i.e., "That *really* turns me on.")

That was my make-or-break list.

Let's work on yours.

First, determine what says, "Husband to the rescue!" to *your* wife. Is it paying the bills? Taking care of her car's maintenance? Driving the kids to school? Vacuuming the house? Unloading the dishwasher? Hopefully you have an idea. If not, try a few on for size and notice how she responds.

When you pull the vacuum out of the front hall closet, does she jump into your arms and wrap her legs around you before you reach the wall outlet? Or, after 10 minutes does she point toward the coffee table and say, "You missed a spot"?

Find out where your greatest return on investment lies.

Next, draft your own make-or-break list similar to the one above. If vacuuming the house was met with a barrage of passionate kisses, and you realize you're on to something, don't just write "vacuum the house" on your list. Spell it out in the first person like I did. How would your wife say it? Why is it important to her? How does it make her feel when you take initiative and pitch in without her having to ask?

For instance:

- "When you vacuum, I know you understand what it takes to keep our home clean and that you're willing to share the load. That makes me feel appreciated." (i.e., "That turns me on.")

Finally, over coffee let your wife know you've been spying on her. Pull out your list and have her review each item. Which ones did you nail? Which ones miss by a mile? What changes would she make? Find out. Take notes. Learn her love language.

She'll wonder who body-snatched her husband.

A-A-A-A-AND … ACTION!

You've done your homework. We *know* you're hot for teacher. Now it's time to put the compound effect to work in your favor.

- Hang your spouse-approved make-or-break list where you'll see it every day (your bathroom mirror or the refrigerator door are good spots). Post another copy prominently in your office or workplace.

- Don't try to tackle every item. What's *one thing* you can do this week to begin moving from zero to hero in the eyes of your wife?

- Excellent. Do it.

- Do it again. A third time. A fourth. Good. Again. It gets easier. A body in motion tends to stay in motion. Again. Soon it'll be second nature.

- Once you've achieved mastery, go back to your list. Pick another item. Repeat.

How do you think your wife will feel once she realizes you're playing for keeps? I don't mean tomorrow. I mean in 31 days. Or maybe a few months.

Loved?

Cherished?

Cared for?

Like a priority to her husband?

How about *all of the above.*

Chances are she'll never say "never" again.

FOR GREATER OOMPH

Read the companion post "Build a Strong and Sexy Marriage with More of These" at wifemagnet.me.

Spice It Up with Leather

Marriage must constantly fight against a monster which devours everything: routine.
−HONORÉ DE BALZAC

Ahhhh, the smell of genuine leather — earthy, elegant, and luxurious. *And the feel* — soft, buttery, and sensuous. There's nothing quite like it. Leather is a game changer! Without it, our sex lives will always be sub-par, and yet astoundingly, only a small fraction of us access its hidden powers. That's about to change.

I was late to the dance. Leather would have saved my marriage. Fortunately, it's saving my life. It became a critical component of my personal transformation last summer when I purchased a leather journal and began writing in it every day.

Let me explain.

My crammed schedule, my no-margin lifestyle, and a glaring lack of maturity kept me from doing the one thing that could have saved my sex life and ultimately, my marriage:

Reflect.

Yes, reflect.

I failed to reflect. I didn't make time to think. To pause. To ask the important questions. Questions like:

- How fulfilled am I in our marriage?

- How would my wife answer that same question?

- When's the last time I wrote a note telling her how much she means to me?

- Getting home in time for dinner is important to her. How did I do this week?

- What's one thing I can do *today* to be a more loving and attentive husband?

- When's the last time I surprised her with a night out or a romantic weekend getaway?

- What's her biggest struggle right now? How can I come alongside her and show my support?

- Where are we "stuck" in our marriage? Who can I call for help?

They were never asked.

Reflect?! Are you kidding?! I had work to do. I had deadlines to meet. I was too busy to get off the hamster wheel.

Consequently, the little things needing to be addressed weren't addressed. The small course corrections needing to be made weren't made. And ever so slightly, my wife began pulling away from me. It wasn't a nuclear bomb that destroyed our sex life. It was a mustard seed. One that grew imperceptibly every passing day.

Lovemaking went from a healthy three times a week, to once a week, to once a month, to … wait for it … three times a year (Valentine's Day, my birthday, and our anniversary). If I had any sense at all, I would have opted out at the once-a-month mark. Let's face it, there's only one thing worse than not having sex, and that's having sex with a woman who looks like she'd rather be doing *anything* else.

A leather journal and a few minutes of reflection each day would have kept my head in the game. It would have helped me be more honest with myself (and with her). It would have helped me be a more thoughtful husband. It would have kept me moving in my wife's direction.

It would have kept us in the three-times-a-week column.

THE PROPER USE OF LEATHER

Journaling isn't difficult. It doesn't require a double major in English composition and comparative literature. It's not staring at a blank page and waiting for inspiration. That's the stuff of bookworms and nerds who write for fun. The journaling I do is simple, targeted, and designed to produce results. Adopted by the world's most successful entrepreneurs and CEOs, it's for everyone who wants to perform at a high level in life and in the bedroom.

I use a helpful little tool called *The Five-Minute Journal.*[7] Go to their website (fiveminutejournal.com) for a visual, but remember, it's not geared toward men who are on the outs with their wives, so until we collaborate and design one, pick up a leather journal at your local bookstore, and I'll show you how simple this is. (If you're against the killing of animals for their hides, imitation leather works just fine.)

START ME UP

Every morning before your day kicks into high gear, find a quiet spot to reflect and answer these three questions (I'll provide sample responses to prime your biggest sex organ — your brain):

1. What's one thing about my wife I'm grateful for?

   I'm grateful for how patient and caring she is with our children.

   If you're pissed-off at her right now and drawing a blank, try this instead:

   What first attracted me to her?

   I was captivated by her beautiful brown eyes. I could have looked into them all night.

2. What's one thing I can do today to be a better husband?

   This morning, before she gets up, I'll clean the pots and pans soaking in the kitchen sink, and prepare a plate of fresh-cut fruit for her and the kids.

3. What's one thing I can do today to communicate my love and appreciation for her?

    I will email her during my lunch break to tell her how much better my life is with her in it.

Every evening before bed, power down your screens and take a few minutes to reflect and answer these three questions:

1. What did I learn today about myself or my wife?

    I think she's been starving for this kind of attention and affection from me for a long time. It feels really good to see her happy.

2. What's one thing I could have done differently today?

    I could have called her from Trader Joe's to see if there was anything she needed while I was there.

3. What do I want to say to her before we fall asleep?

    "I want to have dinner with you this week. Just the two of us. So I can stare into those beautiful brown eyes. How's Friday night?"

Feel how powerful that is? And you're just reading about it. Imagine what it would be like to actually *live* this way. Imagine the damage it would undo. Imagine the impact it would have on the woman you love. Imagine the man you'd become. And imagine what your sex life would morph into. It wouldn't be as good as it used to be, it would be a hundred times better!

Ten days.

Do this for ten days and you'll never go back.

Join the leather crowd.

Safety Nets and Other Life-Saving Devices We Ignore

The one who doesn't tell you what you want to hear,
but tells you what you need to hear. Keep that.

—SONYA TECLAI

Entertainment options were limited when I was a kid. It was the early '70s, the age of plastic dinosaurs, long before Atari and Nintendo walked the earth. Flat screen entertainment consoles and movies on demand were epochs away. We had "TV sets," and available channels numbered in the handfuls, not the hundreds.

My parents compensated by taking us to Madison Square Garden every year to see a circus with a very long name. Dancing bears and lions on leashes weren't really my thing. The annual highlight for me was the high-wire act. I watched awestruck as the trapeze artists risked life and limb, "flying through the air with the greatest of ease," not a safety net in sight. Their aerial acrobatics evoked two visceral reactions inside my eight-year-old chest — reactions most likely shared by you or anyone else who has witnessed their gravity-defying feats (whether in person or on YouTube):

1. "They're amazing!"

2. *"They're nuts!"*

I mean, I have gobs of respect for them, but google "trapeze artist accident" and over 74,000 web pages line up in single file patiently waiting their turn: a loose binding is overlooked, a harness with an invisible hairline fracture gives out, a tiny mid-air miscalculation is made, the guy in the red leotard thinks the guy in the blue leotard checked the safety line. Equipment malfunctions and brief lapses in judgment that result in life-threatening (and life-ending) injuries. Here are just a few of the harrowing headlines:

- 10 Most Horrific Circus Accidents in History
- Trapeze Artist on Life Support after Fall
- Circus of Horrors: Kids Watch Trapeze Artist Fall to His Death
- 9 Performers Injured in 40-Foot Fall
- Cirque du Soleil Acrobat Falls to Her Death During Show Finale

Beyond tragic. At 49, I'm still amazed at what the-best-in-class human beings can do. They inspire me! But all too often, at a great cost to themselves. I just finished watching the edge-of-your-seat documentary *Valley Uprising: Yosemite's Rock Climbing Revolution*. Sadly, one of the sport's pioneers and legends profiled in the film, Dean Potter, died in a wingsuit accident just three weeks after it first aired. As I write this, *Everest* is in theaters. Prior to 1990 and the advent of modern climbing equipment, the fatality rate for attempting to summit the world's tallest peak was 37%. More than one-in-three perished on the mountain. Crazy, right?!

And while no one would fault us for recommending that trapeze artists, BASE jumpers, wingsuit pilots, slackliners, free solo rock climbers, big wave surfers, and mountaineers have their heads examined, let us not forget: "Happily ever after" has an attrition rate upwards of 50%. More than one-in-two marriages is headed for a violent and gruesome death.

Being a husband is risky business.

The biggest difference between modern-day daredevils and us? These exceptional and exacting athletes understand the risks posed by their sport and take all necessary precautions. You and I — in stark contrast — faced with a failure rate exceeding 50%, do nothing.

Who are the *real* nutcases?

"Well, if this one doesn't work out, I can always remarry."

Ha! And you think it's a struggle to breathe *now?!* The divorce rate for second marriages soars to a suffocating 67%. Mountaineers affectionately refer to this as "The Death Zone." You'd be better off joining Wim Hof on his next barefoot, nothing-but-nylon-shorts run to the top of Mt. Kilimanjaro. Your chances of survival are much greater.

CATCH MY FALL

In recent years, the fatality rate for attempting to conquer Everest has plummeted to 5%. "Only" one in twenty die with their climbing boots still on. And it's no accident. Both mountaineers and equipment manufacturers have gotten smarter. It's time for us to clip in and follow their lead.

There *is* a way to substantially reduce your risk exposure as a couple. I was introduced to this simple life-saving device a few years back. Think of it as supplemental oxygen for your marriage. A backup parachute. A safety net. Here's how you rig and install one right in your own home:

1. First, draw up a list of your closest friends and allies. It doesn't have to be long. It might be five deep. It might be seven. It might be ten.

2. Next, narrow it down to two or three men by asking:
   - Who's the most competent?
   - Who places a high value on his marriage?
   - Who talks honestly about his faults?
   - Who's not afraid to challenge me?
   - Who do I trust implicitly?
   - Who am I comfortable sharing the most intimate details of my life with?

   Remember, two or three is plenty. This is your inner circle. This is your Peter, James, and John.

3. Lastly, solicit their help. I recommend doing it face-

to-face at a local tap house. Here's a sample opening statement once pint glasses are comfortably in hand:

"Guys, I've got a favor to ask, but before I do, let me say this: I've had a mediocre marriage for a long time. I've been a mediocre *husband* for a long time. And that's the flattering version. I'm a superstar at work, but I'm Rip Van Winkle at home, sleeping through most of my married life. Distracted. Self-absorbed. Rarely present. My wife wanted a soulmate — instead she got a roommate.

"You can probably tell by the way I'm talking that my long nap is over, thanks to a book that woke me up and pointed me in the right direction. But I'm not stupid … I know building a great marriage isn't easy. We've still got some work to do. And I know myself. There will be times when my buttons get pushed, I get offended, and go total butthead on her. That's where you guys come in: I need you to be my safety net. My search and rescue team in case I go AWOL.

"I want my wife to have the security of knowing there are men she can call on when we're at each other's throats, when our marriage is in a tailspin. She can pick up the phone and say, 'Help! We're hurting! My husband is in a funk, and I can't get through to him. He needs his bros right now. Will you reach out to him?'

"I'm giving her your email addresses and cell phone numbers. I'm gonna tell her I've spoken to you guys, and she has my permission to contact you and disclose whatever she wants. Nothing is out of bounds — how I spend our money, what I say behind closed doors, our sex life — she can rat me out for anything with no fear of retribution. She needs that. *I* need that.

"I trust you guys. You're an important part of my life, my band of brothers. I know you've got my back, and that means a lot to me and my family. Thank you."

Good work. You've just arrived safely back at base camp.

REMOVE THE GAG ORDER

Take your wife to the same tap house. Point out the table where your convocation was held a few days prior. Tell her what you talked about. Be sure to emphasize *why* you're wearing a backup parachute: so she can have the security of knowing you two aren't alone in your marriage. You have friends you're transparent with. Men who know your strengths and weaknesses. Men who are trustworthy. Men who have strong marriages. Men who care deeply about your family. Men who will show up on your doorstep unannounced, with a first-aid kit in one hand and a freshly-sharpened goad in the other, willing to employ whichever the occasion calls for.

A word of caution, however. Next time you're in a sales meeting or on the tee and someone asks about your love life, I suggest curbing your enthusiasm. Don't blurt out, "Hot and steamy ever since I got my three closest friends involved!"

That just sounds wrong.

NEMO RESIDEO

This chapter encapsulates one of the foundational principles this book and my coaching business are built upon:

Men need other men.

You can pretend it's not true. You can ignore it, or run from it, or cover your ears and say, "Blah, blah, blah, I'm not listening." You can even send me nasty emails, or egg my car, or tell your kid to pick on my kid if that statement offends your masculine sensibilities. But whatever you do, get it out of your system, because you're fighting the wrong battle. Climbing Everest is risky.

Climbing it alone is asinine.

The plain and simple truth is: in order to be successful, and do work that matters, and make it to the top — we need each other.

Solomon, Israel's third king, was a man who didn't need much of anything. He had enough silver, gold, horses, chariots, prestige, power, wives, and mistresses to last a thousand lifetimes. Literally. But in spite of all he *did* have, getting out of the lane marked "self-sabotage" required he build friendships with other men. The strong, loyal, we'd-take-an-arrow-for-each-other kind.

Let's examine and dissect one of the proverbs Solomon penned about bromance. It's concise and packed with meaning:

"A friend loves at all times, and a brother is born for adversity."[8]

A friend loves at *all* times

Yes, italics mine, but isn't that the intended emphasis? I think we'd agree friends love us during the good times, when it's easy. That hardly qualifies as a proverb. Solomon, rather, is making a more noteworthy point — a true friend takes the good with the bad. A true friend sticks by our side even when we screw up. Even when we embarrass ourselves. Even when we let others down. A true friend doesn't run for cover when the defecation hits the oscillation, but wades through it with us, no matter how messy it might be.

A brother is born for adversity

Solomon concludes his proverb by leaving no room for doubt. Addressing his captains and soldiers, he cups his hands to his face and shouts, "Men, look around you! Look upon your fellow warriors. Fight for them! Count on them! *Especially* during the heat of battle. *Especially* when the enemy surrounds you. *Especially* when supply lines are cut off. *Especially* when defeat seems imminent. A brother is born for adversity! Nemo Resideo!"

In the book of wisdom known as Ecclesiastes, Solomon would later write:

> "Two are better than one ... If one falls, the other pulls him up; but if a man falls when he is alone, he's in trouble. And one standing alone can be attacked and defeated, but two can stand back-to-back and conquer; three is even better, for a triple-braided cord is not easily broken."[9]

This chapter is what makes all the other ones work. If you're Clark Kent, you can completely ignore it. But if you're a man like me or Solomon, native to the planet, do yourself a solid and take its admonition seriously. Stop trying to impress an invisible jury of your peers; let your guard down and forge vital friendships with other men.

Your wife will thank you. Your children will thank you. *Your sex life will thank you.*

THE LAW OF AVERAGES

I'll wrap up this chapter with a quote from the late Jim Rohn, renowned author and personal-development legend. It's been shared, posted, tweeted, retweeted, written about, blogged, taught, mentioned, and memed around the world. Stare at it for a moment:

> "You are the average of the five people you spend the most time with."

In other words:

- Hang out with five lazy slobs, you'll be the sixth.
- Hang out with five people who barely make ends meet, you'll be the sixth.
- Hang out with five racists, you'll be the sixth.
- Hang out with five people who think bowling is a sport, you'll be the sixth.

It's inevitable. Conversely:

- Hang out with five highly-motivated people, you'll be the sixth.

- Hang out with five millionaires, you'll be the sixth.

- Hang out with five generous and compassionate people, you'll be the sixth.

- Hang out with five guys who eat at Five Guys®, you'll be the sixth.

The lesson here is simple: *Don't* expect to build a world-class marriage if you spend the bulk of your time with guys who wallow in sub-par ones. Better yet, STOP spending time with weak members of the male species who gripe and complain about their marriages. Who never have a kind word to say about their wives. Who are unwilling to look in the mirror. Who hit on other women. Who avoid responsibility by looking at porn.

Or you'll be one of them.

Surround yourself instead with men who refuse to conform with locker room standards. Who work hard at being great husbands. Who acknowledge their flaws. Who get input from other men. Who speak highly of their wives in public. Who install X3watch® on their computers and smart devices. Who have satisfying sex with their own wives.

And you'll be one of them.

It gives new meaning to the term, "friends with benefits."

Better Sex Guarantee #2
-Invite Feedback-

When you talk, you are only repeating what you already know.
But if you listen, you may learn something new.

–THE DALAI LAMA

Blind spots. We all have them. From the least to the greatest. Whether you're Bill Gates, 50 Cent, the Dalai Lama, or a guy who still wears Underoos, none of us are exempt. I have mine. You have yours. They're part of the human condition.

Let's have a look.

First, we all have blind spots that are *physiological:* small areas on each retina without visual receptors. They're responsible for gaps in our field of vision. You wouldn't know it, however, because our brains fill in the missing information using visual cues in the environment. Neat trick.

Second, we all have blind spots that are *psychological:* shortcomings and flaws we're not aware of. These are somewhat more problematic than the optic kind, because we possess no internal mechanism to counterbalance them. Left unchecked, these blind spots create ever-increasing gaps in our field of vision — meaning, our personal deficiencies remain obvious to everyone but us.

The one good thing about psychological blind spots is this: Although they keep *us* in the dark, they're easily identified by others. The next time you're sitting in the bleachers or lounging in the break room, pay attention to the conversation around you. Statements like these are dead giveaways you're in the presence of a married man who needs his side view mirrors adjusted:

- "No matter how hard I try, it's never enough."

- "I work my ass off, what else does she want?"

- "She's not the same woman I married."

- "All she does is _____ (nag, complain, spend my money, etc.)."

- "She's impossible to please."

- "I do *everything* for her. What does she do for me?!"

- "If people knew what I put up with … "

- "This marriage was a mistake."

Can you relate? I sure can. Those words could have easily been spoken by me. I subsisted on a steady diet of denial and chips (the "I'm-all-that-and-a-bag-of" kind) for years. If what leadership guru Ken Blanchard says is true — that feedback is the breakfast of champions — then malnourishment is the reason I had the soul of a weakling.

Feedback wasn't even on my menu.

Now, please understand, I wasn't actively avoiding input or instruction from others, it just never occurred to me I needed it. My vocational proficiency and personal likeability afforded me a steady stream of love and respect from literally thousands of people. I believed my own press for so long that I honestly considered myself a pretty fly husband. I didn't need marriage advice, certainly not from the woman who refused to recognize my vaunted importance and worth.

You already know where that led.

Excelling in any sphere demands we never stop listening to feedback — inviting it, even — especially from the people we're closest to.

NOT SO CHICKEN

No one does this better than Jack Canfield — the highly sought-after success coach, motivational speaker, and co-author of the bestselling *Chicken Soup for the Soul* series. The idea for this chapter arose from something he shared during one of the podcasts in my daily rotation, *Entrepreneur on Fire*. In it, Jack identified one of the essential requirements for all true success: Regular. Constructive. Feedback. Listen to how he applies this in his home:

> "If my wife isn't happy, and I don't ask her for feedback — her mother knows what's wrong with our relationship, her sister knows what's wrong with our relationship, the ladies at the nail salon know what's

wrong with our relationship ... I'm the only one who doesn't know."[10]

To compensate for his blind spots, Jack devised a brilliant way to get consistent feedback from his wife on the state of their union. Every weekend, without fail, he asks her a simple question:

"On a scale of 1-to-10, how would you rate our relationship?"[11]

Any reply less than 10 gets a follow-up question:

"What would it take to make it a 10?"[12]

Every weekend, without fail. I don't know if you're counting, but weekends roll around every seven days or so. While many of us busily avoid our wives on the weekends, hoping to sidestep any dialogue that might bring our character into question, he initiates a game of one-sided Russian roulette with his. This is a very wise man. He knows trust is being built each time he spins the chamber, carefully places the gun barrel to his temple, and gives his wife the floor.

That's called cojones. Cannonball-sized.

Not me. My blind spots were so well-fortified that my poor wife had to endure years of dropping hints, jockeying for position, and cornering me periodically in order to share her deepest wants and needs. Her best chance of getting through to me proved to be in a therapist's office. That's cojones of considerably smaller proportion. BB-sized.

BY INVITATION ONLY

My wife wasn't the only one doomed to a voiceless hell. Most of the women I work with are forced to tiptoe around their husband's fragile ego or risk having acid thrown in their faces. No fun. Hopefully you can understand what a precious gift Jack Canfield bestows upon his wife week in and week out. It's called "permission." Permission to shoot straight. Permission to go out on a limb. Permission to ask for more. Permission to find her voice. Permission she doesn't have to beg, manipulate, entrap or nag him for. It's a gift many married women *never* receive.

"What would it take to make it a 10?"

At face value, it's a straightforward nuts-and-bolts kind of question. Something you'd find on a customer satisfaction survey at the nearest megastore. But look closely and you'll discover it's immeasurably more. This is poetry to a woman's ears. Romance of the highest order. Inspired by the gods. Drawn from the same well that gave birth to *Sleepless in Seattle* and French lingerie.

In fact, it's not a question at all. It's an impassioned plea. Read between the lines and you'll hear Jack trumpet, "Our marriage matters to me! *Nothing* is more important. I'm committed to our success as a couple at any cost. How can I be a better husband? I realize I have blind spots. Tell me where I'm blowin' it. Teach me how to love you. I'm all in!"

Inviting Mrs. Canfield to channel her inner Madonna. To express herself. Every weekend, without fail.

I don't know the man and his wife personally, but it's a good thing they're wealthy. I'm willing to bet they wear out their mattress springs every few months.

LIP-BITERS ANONYMOUS

"What would it take to make it a 10?"

The first time you pose this question to your wife, don't be alarmed if she enters a catatonic state, staring blankly into space, mouthing silent words. Dissociative amnesia and muteness are common symptoms of acute stress response — or "shock" as we like to call it. Calmly repeat the question until color returns to her face. And prepare yourself. Once she regains motor coordination, your significant other will likely have a well-rehearsed suggestion (or two) on how you can up your game in the husband department. That's where this last clip from Jack Canfield comes into play:

> "Here's the thing about feedback: A lot of people give up when they get negative feedback. Some people get mad at the feedback. Some people ignore the feedback. The only response I teach people in my seminars is, 'Thank you for caring enough to share that with me.' Because without feedback, you cannot get better."[13]

That's our goal, isn't it? To grow. To get better. To be the kind of men our wives respect, admire, and get hot and bothered over. Feedback, then, is our trusted friend. The day you stop listening to feedback in your marriage is the beginning of the end. The invisible hand of Fate grabs your checkbook and goes shopping for your burial plot.

"Thank you for caring enough to share that with me."[14]

Do you notice what's missing from Jack's carefully-crafted singular response? There's not a trace of attitude or defensiveness. Not the slightest suggestion of a forthcoming protest. No veiled excuses. He doesn't even express agreement or disagreement, just "Thank you." It's why his approach works so well. Remember, these are uncharted waters for both you *and* your wife. Honest communication feels risky for her, too. No one likes to be sucker punched by their own spouse. What if you get angry and fly off the handle because of something she says? Or turn on her? Or do the passive-aggressive thing and pretend she's invisible for a few days? I hope you have the patience of Job, because she won't be eating cheese from your baited trap again anytime soon.

Instead, do what Jack does. Smile, gently thank her for caring enough to level with you, then change the subject. That's not where this little recon mission ends, of course. Grab your journal and write down everything she said. It's time to devise an actionable plan to move your marriage within striking distance of 10. Using your wife's feedback as a springboard, ask yourself these four questions:

- What needs to change?
- What will I do differently this week?
- How will I track my progress?
- Whose help will I enlist?

Think progress, not perfection. Most women spell *aphrodisiac* e-f-f-o-r-t.

AVOID AUTOPILOT

Granted, this will feel unnatural at first and take some getting used to. Inviting feedback wasn't exactly modeled for us growing up. And lip biting went out of fashion in the '60s. But stick with it. Inviting feedback is a muscle that responds well to the stress and demands of building a great marriage. And while subscribing to Jack Canfield's weekend workout routine is a great place to start, even the *best* fitness plans need to be adjusted every so often in order to keep your muscles guessing. Otherwise, you'll get in a rut and stop growing.

Below are a few dozen questions and conversation starters designed to keep things fresh, eliminate unwanted blind spots, and lead to more impressive gains in your marriage. Think of them as Kegel exercises for your mind. Direct one or two of these toward your wife every few weeks over coffee or cocktails, and you'll outperform every guy in town.

- What do you enjoy most about our marriage?

- What would you like to see us improve?

- What's most challenging about being married to me?

- What's one negative quality of mine I seem to be unaware of?

- What's one thing I do that rubs you the wrong way?

- Where do you feel short changed in our relationship?

- Finish the sentence: "I wish my husband ..."

- If you were to give me one piece of marriage advice, what would it be?

- What are your two biggest concerns about our relationship?

- What are some things I do that make you feel loved and appreciated?

- What mutual goal would you like to see us accomplish?[15]

- How do you like to be kissed?[16]

- How can I best pitch in and help you around the house? With the kids?

- Do you think I spend enough quality time with our children?

- Are you happy with my work schedule? What would you change?

- What do you miss most about the early days of our relationship?

- Is there anything I devote regular time to that you see as a possible threat to our marriage?[17]

- What do you wish we did more of together?

- What are some things I could do to make you feel more secure about us?

- What's something you've explained to me before, but in your opinion I'm still not getting it — you still don't feel heard or understood?

- I'd love to hear about your dreams for the future.[18]

- What's one attribute you'd like me to develop?

- What's one attribute you'd like me to help *you* develop?

- What can I do to better support you and your dreams?

- Do you think we have enough fun together?

- What would you change about how we manage our money?

- How are you doing health-wise? Do you have any concerns?

- If you could change one thing about our priorities as a family, what would it be?[19]

I doubt you're in danger of it, but don't let one or two-word answers suffice. For example, if you pose the question, "What do you wish we did more of together?" and she answers "Have fun," probe a little deeper. Try, "Give me an example," or "What does 'have fun' look like to you?" The goal is to get inside her head. If it feels vaguely familiar — like you're courting her all over again — you're on the right track.

GO FOR THE GOLD

Years ago my wife and I attended a two-day Couples Communication Class taught by a dynamic husband-and-wife team of social psychologists, Sherod and Phyllis Miller. Over the course of a weekend, they instructed couples on the finer points of two groundbreaking skills arcane to most marriages: how to talk, and how to listen. I'm not kidding. A few hours in their presence left me scratching my head in disbelief, faced with the realization I sucked at both.

I want to zero-in on a critical point they emphasized to all the husbands in the room: When conversation is winding down and it *appears* your wife is finished talking … she's not finished talking. She has more to say. Note, this is after you've invited feedback. After you've listened intently. After you've acknowledged her feelings. After you've probed a little deeper. After you've listened some more. This is after her martini glass is empty. After she's smiled warmly across the table at you. After she's asked for the check.

She has more to say.

And it's not, "They make good martinis here." No, the card she's been holding close to her chest, the thing she's hesitated to talk to you about, *needs* to be talked about. It's vitally important to the health of your marriage and your closeness as a couple.

That's where this seemingly innocuous but oh-so-powerful little question comes in. Remember, it doesn't get asked until the conversation is all but over, until *after* she's asked for the check. Here's how you call her bluff:

> "Is there anything else you want to tell me?"

Ask it thoughtfully. Ask it lovingly. Then sit still and be quiet.

This is how you hit pay dirt. This is how, in the words of our seasoned instructors, you *"get to the gold."* The "gold" could be any number of things. It might be a personal struggle she feels safe to share. Or an idea for a business she secretly wants to start. It might be a story of abuse from her past. Or a confession of guilt. It might be, "I think I'm ready to forgive you for the affair." Maybe it's an honest admission of what's *really* been bothering her. It might even be her chance to say, "I want to be a better wife."

Whatever the case, take your shoes off. You're standing on holy ground.

Better Sex Guarantee #3
-Agree with Her-

How can a woman be expected to be happy with a man who insists on treating her as if she were a perfectly normal human being.

—OSCAR WILDE

Part of the genius of Jack Canfield's weekly ritual is *he* gets to pick when to approach his wife for feedback. He heads into each conversation mentally prepared in case she opens a can. Plus, as every married couple knows, timing is everything. What's her emotional state? Is she calm or agitated? Smiling or scowling? Content or coming apart at the seams? There are good times and bad times to discuss the finer points of your relationship. Right after bringing her breakfast in bed is probably a good time. Right after commenting on the weight she's gained probably isn't.

In case it's not obvious, the purpose of engaging her while she's in her happy place isn't to skew the results, but to increase the likelihood you'll get feedback that's valuable and useful. It also serves to minimize your risk of personal injury. It's the same reason our military personnel sweep for landmines before advancing into unfamiliar territory. Inviting feedback is a learned skill.

WHEN OPPORTUNITY COST KNOCKS

Invariably, there are times when you're on the receiving end of marital input that's *un*-invited. You know the kind. It comes out of nowhere, typically preceded by "you always," or "you never," and feels more like a personal attack than constructive we're-on-the-same-team criticism. It's the shower scene from *Psycho*, except you're the one being sliced to ribbons.

My custom was to politely excuse myself from conversations like these, and by "politely excuse," I mean leap from the nearest window. Occasionally, I wrestled the chef's knife from her hand and lashed back.

What a fool I was! Moments like these — when we're naked, defenseless, and hemorrhaging blood — afford us our greatest opportunities for advancement and reward. Failing to recognize this has already cost us untold millions in marital capital.

You're about to learn why being ambushed and savagely dismembered by your wife is better than finding a $100 bill, meeting the president, or sitting in the owner's box on Super Bowl Sunday. Never again will you fear being blindsided.

You'll actually *welcome* it.

CUE GARY COLEMAN

Our next sound bite comes from the hills of northern Israel, spoken by Jesus many centuries ago. He had a lot to say about relationships, blind spots, and situational awareness. His parable of the person who points out a speck of sawdust in someone else's eye, while oblivious to the plank in his own, is world-famous. Here's an excerpt from Matthew's Gospel that's not as familiar, but contains enough electrical current to resuscitate your unresponsive sex life. It's taken from a translation called The Expanded Bible:

> "If your enemy [opponent; adversary; accuser] is taking you to court, become friends [reach agreement; settle matters] quickly, before you go to court. Otherwise, your enemy might turn you over to the judge, and the judge might give you to the guard to put [throw] you in jail. I tell you the truth, you will not leave there until you have paid everything you owe [the last penny]."[20]

Wordy, I know, but stick with me. We're going somewhere important. I'm not a theologian and don't purport to be, so let's dismount from the high horse of religion and plant our feet on terra firma. Jesus, after all, spent most of his time hanging out with ordinary knuckleheads like us. Here's my paraphrase of what He's saying to sex-starved husbands:

> "If your wife accuses you of something, agree with her."[21]

[Insert sound of record scratch here.]

Whatchu talkin' 'bout, Jesus?

Yup, agree with her.

Her tone sucks...I know. Her words are sharp...I know. She's exaggerating...I know. Her facts aren't accurate...I know. She doesn't make sense … I know. You're not as bad as she's making you out to be … I know. You don't deserve to be butchered like this in the comfort of your own bathtub… I know. I get it! I really do.

But when your wife goes judge, jury, and executioner on you, Jesus said you only have two radically-opposing options to choose from:

1. Defend yourself
2. Agree with her

Although its prospects are bleak, option number one is the choice of lunkhead and foot-shooting husbands everywhere. I was one of them. A man on a mission to prove Jesus wrong. Fortunately, "I told you so" isn't part of his vocabulary, because the way I handled my wife's unwelcome performance appraisals consistently produced the outcome Jesus predicted: more time in solitary confinement and a sex life that resembled stale crusts of moldy bread. To add insult to injury, I was also classified as a "habitual offender" and lost all credit for time served.

Option number two, according to Jesus, is much more promising. Quickly agreeing with your wife when you feel attacked is similar to injecting her with a mild sedative. It produces an immediate "calming" effect, rendering her susceptible to feeling favorable toward you again, even introducing the possibility of make-up sex.

At the very least, it affords you the opportunity of a fair trial.

NO WIMPS ALLOWED

I'm not suggesting you practice up on your "look-at-me-I'm-a-doormat" skills, or offer your manhood on the altar of appeasement. I'm not advocating you mutate into a lower life form and become the proverbial sniveling, spineless, "Yes, dear" husband. That's not what Jesus said, and it's not what I'm saying. Jesus is inviting us into strong-man territory, not sissified air. Here, rather, is what he's advising us:

When your wife has a criticism or complaint against you, *agree with the part that's true.*

You can do that.

Oh, you may not appreciate her tone. Or her choice of words. Maybe she's nitpicking. Maybe her accusations are unfair. Maybe she's guilty of much worse. That might all be true, but is there something about what she's saying you can agree with?

Something?!

It doesn't have to be 100%. It might only be 25%, or even 10%. But *something.* Is there *something* you can agree with? Even if it's a molehill and not the mountain she's made it out to be. Is there even a tiny shred of truth to what you stand accused of? Look past her tone and delivery. Is there *something* you can take responsibility for? Is there something — *even one thing* — you can acknowledge?

There always is.

And the moment you identify it and own it is the moment you

start acting like a man. It's the moment you charge the tower and slay the dragon and rescue the princess. You couldn't have known this, but she's been desperately waiting for the sound of your steed, anticipating the day you'd come to carry her away from that lonely and forsaken place. Because the moment you agree with your wife and say, "You know something... you're right" is the moment she realizes she's not actually crazy.

> "I'm not crazy?! I knew it ... I *knew* it! I'm not crazy! I'm going to be OK. *We're* going to be OK. I'm not crazy! Ha ha ha ha ha ha ..."

You've lifted the weight of a thousand worlds off her shoulders. With one small admission, you've relieved her (finally) of the terrible burden of bitchiness she's been forced to carry. Life returns to normal. *She* returns to normal. Your wife is back. The kind, caring, and tender woman you married all those years ago.

The one who had to be strong because you weren't.

BEST DIRECTOR NOMINATION

Let me illustrate why this method of handling unwelcome criticism produces such dramatic results. Here's a real-life example from my own marriage: Imagine it's a few minutes shy of 8:00 p.m. I've just walked in the door after spending too many hours at the office. My wife is locked and loaded.

Take 1

Me: "Honey, I'm home."

My Wife: "You know what?! I'm *sick* of you working late every night! You're never here when we sit down to eat. I don't know why I even bother to cook for you!"

Me: "Are you kidding?! That is s-o-o-o not true! I don't work late *every* night. Last week I left the office on time and got home for dinner on Tuesday *and* Friday. You don't remember that, do you? No, of course not. And why am *I* always the one who gets picked on for being late?! What about you?! A few days ago you were late for our meeting with blah blah blah blah … "

Nice shot, Jeff. How does your foot feel?

Now, keep in mind, my response was entirely factual. Technically speaking, I was more "right" than my wife was. The week prior I really did leave the office on time Tuesday and Friday. I really did sit down and enjoy dinner with my family, as I so clearly pointed out. And she really was late for a meeting with our financial advisor a few days prior. All of that was true. If you'd been in the room, I would've extended my arm in your direction for a fist bump. I was a shrewd defense attorney but a harebrained husband. "Winning the argument" and "being more factually correct" were misguided goals. I only pushed my wife further and further away.

I "won" the debate, yes, but lost her respect. I lost her trust. I lost her admiration. And *we* kept losing ground in our marriage. And in our bedroom. In every room, for that matter. I was the king of fools. Brand this on your brain with a hot iron: *Even if you win, you lose.* Oh, you might back your wife into a corner and win the argument, but the box score will still read "L."

OK, let's re-shoot the scene above. Imagine Jesus walks through the wall of our home, yells "Cut!" and hands me a revised script.

Take 2

> **Me:** "Honey, I'm home."
>
> **My Wife:** "You know what?! I'm *sick* of you working late every night! You're never here when we sit down to eat. I don't know why I even bother to cook for you!"

It's here on the page where Jesus scribbled a few notes for my benefit:

> "Jeff, although this angry outburst is directed at you, it's not a personal attack. Your wife is in pain. So instead of standing up for yourself, *man up* and listen to what she's *really* saying. What she's desperately trying to say is, 'The days are long and I miss you and I don't know why you won't spend more time with me and I wish you cared more about us and I still hold out hope that one day you will but right now I hate my life because I feel alone in our marriage and all I do is cook and clean for a husband who only notices me when he wants sex.' "

Lucky for me, Jesus knows how to speak female.

So this time, instead of raising my deflector shields and preparing for the Battle of Naboo, I take a softer, more calculated, "I'm-tired-of-sleeping-on-the-couch" approach. With some much needed direction from Jesus, I agree with the part of my wife's complaint that's true, address the *real* source of her pain, and treat this moment as an opportunity to mend what's broken in our marriage.

> **Me:** "You know something...you're right. We only had dinner together as a family twice last week, and truthfully, that sucks. Getting home on time needs to be the rule and not the exception. I have a meeting with my boss tomorrow. I'm going to tell him I can't keep this up. Our marriage is too important. And you know what? I'm way overdue for a day off. Why don't I ditch work this Friday? We can go out for coffee...take a walk on the beach...whatever you want. It's been awhile since we've had an 'us' day, and I'm needing one. How about you?"

Holy 1975 Arnold Schwarzenegger! That's raw power I just unleashed! It's called the power of agreement. The power of building a bridge instead of widening the divide. The power of taking her side. The power of *helping my wife feel heard.*

According to the National Center for Health Statistics, women are the ones who file for divorce close to 70% of the time. Those surveyed cited "not feeling heard" as one of the primary reasons they leave the men they love. You read that right — the men they love.

This thing is no joke.

THE JEKYLL AND HYDE DIFFERENCE

You know when you're in the presence of a woman who feels heard by her husband. She's graceful. She's magnetic. She's fun to be around. Catch her during a "didn't-have-time-to-put-on-makeupoh-well" trip to the grocery store, and she still turns heads.

Take the exact same woman and confine her to a marriage where she *doesn't* feel heard, and you'll be forced to watch in horror as she contracts a case of the uglies. Over time you'll hardly recognize her. I witnessed this transformation in my own home. As I grew less empathetic and more defensive as a husband — sticking to the old script — my attractive, model-looks wife morphed into a homely woman. Being married to me literally drained the life out of her. She began showing up with greater frequency as Mrs. Hyde — her angrier, uglier, contempt-ridden alter ego. And just like the character in Robert Louis Stevenson's novella, the longer she stayed married to me, the more she feared her transformation would be permanent unless she left for good.

If your wife doesn't feel heard, it's likely she's been wrestling over the same two agonizing choices I presented mine: the pain of breaking up our family, or the pain of remaining a grotesque version of her once-beautiful self. Your wife deserves better. It's time to present her with a third option: a brand *new* story. A story resembling the one she scripted and rehearsed as a little girl. A story where knights aren't perfect, but still wear shining armor and still fight for the hearts of the women they love.

Women who feel heard in their marriages:

- Smile more
- Laugh more
- Look 10 years younger than those who don't

- Buy lingerie more frequently than those who don't

- Glow

- Experience a deep sense of connection with their husbands

- Are much slower on the draw

- Feel loved

- Feel cherished

- Feel sexy

- Feel like they matter

- Throw fewer tantrums

- Like to play dress-up

- Forgive their spouses when they blow it

- And hardly ever wear their scary-old-lady-from-the-Bates-Motel wig

Agreeing with your wife helps her feel heard. It brings out the best in her. It's like throwing a pail of water on her wicked-witch-of-the-west tendencies. Try it and see for yourself. She may not melt into your arms then and there, but she *will* lie in bed later that night re-evaluating her "punish-husband-by-withholding-sex" strategy. She might even open her soul a smidge and risk letting you back in. It's what women who feel heard do.

Jesus knew what the hell he was talking about.

Women and the Fine Art
of Door Slamming

*If you're willing to do only what's easy, life will be hard.
But if you're willing to do what's hard, life will be easy.*

—T. HARV EKER

In many ways, my wife and I were a perfect fit. She's a little bit country, I'm a little bit rock and roll. She's big picture, I'm fine print. She's spontaneous, I'm routine. She slams doors, I tiptoe past them. We had the potential to be a formidable team.

My wife wasn't always a door-slammer. It's a skill she learned later in life — shortly after meeting me, to be precise. Prior to our relationship, she was a loving mom and successful businesswoman who communicated effectively without the assistance of loud and jarring noises to emphasize a point.

THE TIPPING POINT

Door slamming wasn't an everyday occurrence in our home, and it certainly wasn't my wife's preferred weapon of choice. But during heated exchanges, with volleys being launched by both sides, she would occasionally end an argument by storming out of the room, marching upstairs, and slamming our bedroom door behind her.

Looking back, I can't blame her. She felt mostly unheard in our marriage. I was frustrating to live with. I was frustrating to fight with. My former combat style could be summarized as "never give an inch." So when her feminine intuition, like a drone flying overhead, determined with pinpoint accuracy I was acting like a complete ass and unwilling to budge, she discharged her weapon of last resort. BOOM!

Argument over.

What happened next is the real crime: I went about my business.

You see, when my wife grabbed our bedroom door with both hands, wound up, and made all the windows in our home rattle, I assumed it meant, "*Get away from me!*"

Not even close.

What it *really* meant, as I would later learn, was "*Come after me! Fight for me like you used to!*"

We weren't taught this in school. Heck, I spent 12 weeks in premarital counseling and door slamming wasn't mentioned even once.

THE SOUND OF SILENCE

In the early '90s I had a front row seat for the separation and divorce of a very dear couple. (He's still like a brother to me.) In the third year of their marriage, my buddy flew from L.A. to Dallas for a business trip. When he arrived home a few days later, their apartment was empty and she was gone. No note, no furniture, no food in the cupboard. *Sayonara, baby!* Come to find out, she had recruited her brother to drive down from Sacramento, rent a U-Haul, and load up her things. My friend, to put it lightly, was crushed. I was there for the fallout.

Here's the odd thing: as decisive, well-planned, and well-executed as her actions appeared, she took her time filing for divorce. Months went by before she made up her mind. Can you guess why? Take a stab at it. She was waiting for something. More specifically, for some*one*. After refusing to speak with her husband over the phone hundreds of times, here's the reason she finally gave him for ending their marriage, her exact words:

"You didn't come after me."

He called her. He paged her. He left messages. Long ones. Short ones. Passionate ones. He read from his journal. He recited their entire scrapbook of love letters and cards. He swallowed his pride and called her father — numerous times — pleading for a chance to speak with her. Just once. *Please! Just once!*

And she relented. Just once. Long enough to say:

"You didn't come after me."

She was right. It was the one thing he didn't do. He didn't go after her. He should have. He should have dropped everything. He should have slept in her father's front yard à la Nicolas Cage in *Valley Girl*, howling at the moon and hollering her name at the top of his lungs. She was, after all, just a stone's throw up the Golden State Freeway, a measly 403 miles away. Love has scaled *much* higher walls. He could have eaten an early breakfast and been there by noon.

He didn't, but for very "good" reasons — new clients, deadlines, deals to close, a clunker for a car. I mean, what if he broke down in the Central Valley, on that monotonous stretch of drought-stricken wilderness, interrupted only by slaughterhouses and almond fields? Or, what if he made it all the way to Sacramento only to find out she wouldn't see him, wouldn't even come to the door? What a waste of time *that* would be.

He left voicemails instead.

She didn't hear a single one. Oh, she listened to them all, but the only thing she heard was:

"I'm not coming after you. You're not worth fighting for."

And so it went: each time her pager chirped for attention, each time her cordless phone burst into song, serenading her with Vivaldi's "Spring," each time her answering machine blinked anxiously from across the room, its computerized voice announcing, "You have four new messages," and each time she awoke to an empty front yard — a patch of grass where her shivering and unshaven husband should have been — that broken record took one more trip around the turntable:

"I'm not coming after you. You're not worth fighting for."

It's what my wife heard in the wake of each slammed door, as she stood with bated breath hoping I'd give chase, hoping I'd come after her. Nope. I went on with my day. I got something to eat. I rode my mountain bike. I worked in the garage. I ran errands.

"I'm not coming after you. You're not worth fighting for."

Whispered in the sounds of silence.

Dumbass husband.

Little did I know dark and sinister storm clouds were gathering over our home. For it was in those moments — when she was left feeling abandoned and alone — that "a vision softly creeping, left its seeds while I was sleeping."[22] She began to fantasize about leaving me. She began to dream about love, and laughter, and dancing, and date nights, and walks on the beach with a man who knew about slammed doors. The subtle idea she'd be better off with someone else began to slowly take root, until it was planted in her brain.

Permanently.

I remember the day the tempest made landfall and reached our home. It was the day I realized she wasn't coming back. The day I learned another had taken my place.

Hello darkness, my old friend.[23]

ALL HAIL THE QUEEN!

The movie *Taken* doesn't show up on anyone's "Top 100 Chick Flicks of All Time." Makes sense, considering its backdrop is the underbelly of human trafficking. Plus, the film is bereft of cuddling, puppies, and gut-wrenching breakups. And, worth mentioning, violent deaths outnumber romantic gestures 80 to 1.

So then, *why?* Why do women swoon over it? Why do all the girly girls I know love this smash-bang ode to Jason Bourne? *Why has my own mother seen it over a dozen times?!*

I'll give you a clue: The answer is found in the film's climactic scene, where Liam Neeson's character calmly puts a slug through the head of the dirtbag who paid for his daughter's virginity. Do you remember what Kim says to her father in that moment, as her would-be rapist falls dead to the floor? Every woman who's seen it does. Four simple words crowning *Taken* the undisputed queen of all chick flicks. Watch it again and listen closely. Right before collapsing into her father's arms, right before the dam bursts, through reined-in tears of astonishment and untold relief, Kim chokes back emotion just long enough to sputter:

> *"You came for me."*[24]

Understand that one line, and you'll understand the soul and longing of every woman — to be loved, to be pursued, to be fought for.

From now on, no matter what's on the other side, you'll bravely open slammed doors, not tiptoe past them.

[**Note:** Some women substitute door slamming with the silent treatment. Others get in the car, screech out of the driveway, and hunker down with a relative or close friend for a few days. Whatever the case, the same principle applies — Go after her!]

FOR GREATER OOMPH

Read the companion post "The Warrior Gets the Girl" at wifemagnet.me.

The "A" Word

It's hardly talked about. It's a word that, unfortunately, has "stigma" written all over it. Yet most women have been wounded by this beast more than once, often before they're old enough to tie their own shoes.

It crept into my wife's home when she was just four years old. The day her father left for good. She cried for him every night during most of her little-girl life. Apart from the occasional sugar-daddy visit and photo op, he stayed away for forty, long, soul-crushing years.

It showed up in the life of a close friend at the tender age of seven, when a five-year cycle of molestation at the hands of her own father began. Abuse that's hard to fathom. But to this day, her deepest anger is directed toward her mother. The one who *knew* about the evil in their home, but didn't lift a finger to stop it.

Abandoned by dad. Abandoned by mom. Wounds that run deep.

Some escape childhood unscathed and aren't preyed upon until they're teenagers. Or twenty-somethings. Much like the blue-skinned shapeshifter Mystique of *X-Men* lore, the supervillain named Abandonment can appear in a variety of forms throughout a woman's life:

- Used
- Dumped
- Lied to
- *He told me he loved me*
- Cheated on
- Betrayed
- Left at the altar
- Jilted
- Dropped
- Smeared
- Shunned
- *I thought we were friends*
- Passed up
- Neglected
- Discarded
- Forgotten

Abandonment's list is long.

So are its tentacles. Without expert help, these same tentacles remain deeply embedded throughout adulthood. I'm not suggesting your wife is damaged goods, but if she's ever been A-worded, if she's ever been hung out to dry by someone she trusted, even if it was forty years ago, the impact of that event *still* speaks to her. Don't think it doesn't affect your marriage, it already has! That story of never coming through got there a long time before you did. It's why the scales of justice in your home are tipped against you. You're paying, in part, for someone else's sins.

50 WAYS TO LEAVE YOUR LOVER

In the early days of our marriage, lurking under the surface, resided my wife's greatest fear: the fear of being abandoned. I didn't know it. I wasn't aware of it. But he was there. Loathsome creature who had defiled her more than once.

Instead of being a source of healing to the woman I loved, I unwittingly joined the ranks of those who had left her. Instead of holding Abandonment at gunpoint and running it out of our home, I became one of its faithful envoys.

- I worked obscenely long hours, leaving home as the sun rose and often returning hours after it had set.

- I canceled date nights.

- I worked on my days off.

- On the infrequent family vacation, I snuck work into my suitcase like an unwelcome stowaway.

- I gave my best time and energy to other people.

- I made promises I didn't keep.

- I came through for others, but not for her.

And I said *"I'll change"* so often, my words weighed less than a dryer sheet.

All this from the guy who promised to *never* leave her. Who promised to love her and pursue her and fight for her heart. By the time she withdrew emotionally and sexually, I had been gone for years, I just couldn't see it. My cone kept getting in the way. I came unglued the day it dawned on me:

- My absence was the same as leaving her.

- Giving my best energy to my career was the same as leaving her.

- Working on my days off was the same as leaving her.

- Failing to take her side in a conflict was the same as leaving her.

- My inattentiveness as a husband was the same as leaving her.

- Promising so much but delivering so little was the same as leaving her.

Worst of all, I labeled her *overreactive* and pouted when she refused to eat my leftovers.

DR. SPOCK ON THE DANCE FLOOR

A photo from our wedding day still haunts me. It's our first dance. We're swaying to Shania Twain beneath eucalyptus trees draped in twinkly lights:

> From this moment life has begun
> From this moment you are the one
> Right beside you is where I belong
> From this moment on
>
> I give my hand to you with all my heart
> Can't wait to live my life with you, can't wait to start
> You and I will never be apart
> My dreams came true because of you[26]

My wife's eyes are fastened on mine. And the expression on her face is exquisite. So tender. So trusting. So hopeful. It's her left hand that ruins me. Her fingers are clenched around my shoulder in a Vulcan death grip. It's as if, in that moment, her four-year-old self was pleading, "Don't *you* leave me. Don't *you* stop loving me. Don't *you* stop choosing me." She was clinging for dear life. My poor bride must have known intuitively she was doomed to a fate Helen Rowland so aptly described:

> "When a girl marries, she exchanges the attention of many men for the inattention of one."

Looking back, "Dancing with Myself" would have been much more appropriate.

THE *OTHER* "A" WORD

I've noticed something about sex books. 99% of them are "How To" manuals. Skills to hone. Outfits to wear. Positions to try. Places to try them. And yet, as a coach who works with couples, not a single woman has ever said to me, "My interest in sex has cooled because my husband isn't willing to experiment."

Not one.

But they do talk.

- They talk about feeling emotionally abandoned.

- They talk about the pain of being a work widow.

- They talk about a lack of meaningful connection.

- They talk about feeling neglected. Or taken for granted.

And the word I hear most often?

Alone.

"I feel alone in my marriage."

That's when their eyes well up.

WRONG IS THE NEW RIGHT

Due to her wiring, a woman can't stomach being ignored. It runs counter to every cell in her body. A woman needs to be *noticed*. Not just when she's dressed to the nines and looking her best. But when she's gardening. Or doing lunges. Or curled up on the couch with a novel. She needs her husband to *see her* when she's folding laundry. Or blending a smoothie. Or sitting on the floor hunched over pink foam toe separators.

Ask any therapist — the majority of women who check out of their marriages, have affairs, and eventually leave their husbands aren't bad people. They're just people who lost heart. People who grew weary waiting in line.

I know a few dozen women who have cheated. First-timers. For the most part, they're caring wives, attentive moms, and loved by their in-laws. None are the conniving, backstabbing, watch-out-for-that-little-hussy kind. And while the circumstances vary, the stories are the same: Each one married a man who stopped noticing her. Stopped noticing her good qualities. Stopped noticing the sparkle in her eyes reserved just for him. And stopped noticing the red flags she began hoisting with greater frequency.

Cones will do that.

A client of mine, a married woman of otherwise high moral character, had a passionate year-long affair. She said to me, "I know what I did was wrong, but at the time, it didn't *feel* wrong. It didn't *feel* like cheating." Can you wrap your head around that? I can. No, I'm not defending her or the choices she made. It wasn't OK to cheat — to hide and lie and hurt her husband so deeply. But to her, a woman gasping for air and barely treading water in a capsized marriage, cheating didn't feel like cheating. It felt like getting rescued at sea.

Another woman I work with said, "Yes, I have flaws. But I'm also strong and creative and mysterious and beautiful. I wanted someone to see beyond my flaws and notice my beauty … notice *me*."

Someone did.

Another lamented, "I just wanted to be attractive to someone." Mind you, this comes from the mouth of a very accomplished, good-looking, and secure woman. What do you think she really wanted? Someone to pay her a compliment? Someone to "like" her profile picture? Someone to say, "I think you're pretty"? Hardly. Her husband thinks she's pretty. Most men would consider her attractive. No, what she meant was, "I just wanted to *matter* to someone. I just wanted to be a *priority* to someone. I just wanted to be *wanted* by someone."

In his seminal book, *Wild at Heart,* John Eldredge contends women are designed this way. They need to be noticed, to be seen, to be wanted — especially by the two most important men in their lives.

> "Most little girls will remember playing dress up, or wedding day, or 'twirling skirts,' those flowing dresses that were perfect for spinning around in. She'll put her pretty dress on, come into the living room and twirl. What she longs for is to capture her daddy's delight. My wife remembers standing on top of the coffee table as a girl of five or six, and singing her heart out. *Do you see me?* asks the heart of every girl. *And are you captivated by what you see?*"[27]

30 or 40 years later … she's still asking.

Whether your wife wears flowing dresses or not, it's time to put your iPad down and notice her. That grown-up little girl you married is standing on the coffee table for a reason, and if you don't see her, someone else will.

Women on tables *always* get noticed.

FACEBOOK IS YOUR MORTAL ENEMY

When I was a kid, married women escaped the boredom of stay-at-home-housewife purgatory by indulging in romance novels and soap operas. Not anymore. Today, sitting at the kitchen table with a laptop or smartphone, they can interact and emote with real people.

For the first time in history, we're competing against "likes." A woman can post a photo of the rosemary garlic chicken she just took out of the oven and have no less than 30 "likes" and a dozen "Looks delicious!" comments before her husband even has the chance to sit down and eat.

So, what's the answer? Set your smartphone notifications to "electric shock" mode and one-up her friends' comments with a few warm fuzzies of your own? I don't think so. Here's the point: Other people are paying close attention to your wife and connecting with her in meaningful ways. *Are you?* Because if you're not, you're losing ground every week.

I know men who are easily irritated when their insignificant other spends "too much time" chatting online. I witnessed one guy openly berate his wife over it. I don't think she heard him, even though the cone around his head amplified his words and made it sound like he was in charge. Unfazed, she stopped watching *Dancing with the Stars* just long enough to shake her head and mutter "You idiot …" under her breath.

An hour later over a Guinness, I listened to this husband's complaints, pulled out a scratch pad, and guided him through a few questions:

- What is my wife getting from online interaction that she's not getting from me?

- Which of her *legitimate emotional needs* — to feel important, loved, appreciated, admired, included, cared for, supported, listened to, noticed, needed, recognized, respected, valued, and understood — go unmet in our marriage?

I'm not ruling out the possibility (although it's slight) your wife has a Facebook addiction. But there's a much higher probability social media is her husband-by-proxy. It's also your early warning system, your amber "50 miles to empty" light. Because unless something changes, romance and sex are the next two needs she'll outsource.

THE REAL WAR ON WOMEN

Have you heard the joke about the genie who changes his mind? It goes something like this:

> A guy is walking on the beach in Southern California when he finds an old brass lamp. As he rubs it, a genie pops out and says, "For letting me out of my lamp, I

will grant you one wish — whatever you'd like." Without thinking, the guy spouts, "Build me a bridge to Hawaii! I've always wanted to vacation there, but I'm deathly afraid of flying."

Taken aback, the genie protests, "*A bridge to Hawaii?! That's over 2,500 miles away! Do you realize how deep the ocean floor is? Imagine how much concrete and steel I'd need just to support it, much less build it! I've never turned down a wish before, but I'm sorry, you'll have to come up with something more reasonable.*"

The guy thinks for a moment and says, "I want to be able to understand my wife. I want to know how to make her happy."

Without missing a beat the genie replies, "Do you want that bridge with two lanes or four?"

You can laugh, it is funny. But is it *true?* We certainly snicker and act like it is. *But is it?* Is this really the fate of every husband? To live in perpetual darkness, never knowing what makes his wife happy? Is it *true* women are impossible to understand? Impossible to figure out? Will it *always* be a roll of the dice?

Or … is this the Propaganda Machine at work? A brazen ploy to sidestep responsibility. A calculated effort to elicit sympathy, suppress the opposition, and divert attention away from the cones we wear. I mean, what if the genie joke was spread by the same apparatus that put "A woman's place is in the kitchen" and "Men don't talk about their feelings" into circulation?

Humor me for a minute. What if the opposite is true? What if the key to a woman's heart has been staring us in the collective face for millennia, and we've been too lazy to notice? What if your wife isn't the frighteningly unpredictable Pacific, with its mile-deep canyons and trenches? What if she's the gurgling creek in the woods behind your house — the one you can cross in a single step? And what if making her happy is found in three simple words the Propaganda Machine has been hiding from you since puberty? Three simple words that will bring the A-word behemoth to its knees and launch your sex life into the stratosphere.

BACK TO THE FUTURE

Before I reveal the secret sauce, there's a video we need to watch.

It's your wedding day.

The people you love most are gathered under one roof. Look at how decked out everyone is! Even your five-year-old nephew is killing it in his tiny blue blazer. And the smiles … none were bigger than hers that day.

And there you are, standing up front with your hands crossed, waiting for her grand entrance. Close your eyes and try to remember how you felt when those massive wooden doors swung open, the first notes of her bridal march were struck, and God's crowning achievement walked down the aisle, beaming as she placed her hands in yours. What a powerfully symbolic moment! She was saying goodbye to family, friends, former lovers, potential suitors, her independence — life as she knew it — so she could give herself completely to you and the life you'd create *together*.

Skip past the preacher's niceties and fast forward to the vows. You went first. You were the lead-off batter. Wow! Those are some serious promises you made. And notice how her vows, although heartfelt, were made in response to yours. Her commitment to love and cherish *you* was predicated upon your commitment to love and cherish *her*. That's foundational to the contract. Now, just thinking out loud here: I wonder how she would have responded had the officiant asked, "Do you promise to put your life on hold — to cook for him, clean for him, do his laundry, iron his shirts, raise his children, have enthusiastic sex, and completely ignore the attention of other men in exchange for an occasional distracted date night — even if he stops making you a priority? Even if it means feeling alone in your marriage … so help you God?"

Good thing he didn't have a crystal ball.

The scene I most want you to see takes place during the reception. The DJ has just cleared the parquet floor in the center of the room. Its only inhabitants are you and your glowing bride. The song you picked for your first dance begins to play. You probably haven't heard it in a while, so pay close attention to the words. They embody how she felt that day, what she envisioned for your future, what she wanted for your marriage, and deep down, what she *still* wants. I'm guessing her posture toward you is very different right now, but like a seed waiting for moisture and sunlight, those dormant feelings can quickly spring back to life.

As your first dance winds down, pick a spot in the video where her face is in full view and pause it there. Look closely at her eyes — so tender, so trusting, so hopeful. *This is the person who bet it all on you.* What you can't see (and what you couldn't have known at the time) is that behind those eyes, buried in the recesses of her cerebral cortex where long-term memories are stored, a faint cry fought for attention: "You won't abandon me, will you? You won't get busy and forget about me, will you? You won't stop choosing me, will you?"

Make no mistake, that *is* what this is all about — the dance, the dress, the DJ, the guests, the photos, the flowers, the champagne, the hors d'oeuvres, the cake, the bridal shower, the rehearsal dinner, the limo, the gifts, the rings, the tuxes, the toasts, even the pan-seared halibut with citron beurre blanc sauce — you chose her.

You chose her.

To be fair, she had a say in the matter, and you didn't choose her right away, of course. You noticed her first. It may have been while standing in line at Staples, or jogging the grassy median along San Vicente, or riding the down escalator into the Whole Foods at Columbus Circle. But regardless of when and where, you *saw* her. And you figured out a way to keep seeing her. Weeks turned into months, until the day came when you chose her. You didn't arrive here lightly, so you bought a ring that cost you something. A ring that conveyed the weight of your life-altering decision: "This is the person I love more than any person I've ever loved. This is the woman I want to spend and share the rest of my life with." Then you presented the ring as proof, along with a short speech, of your decision to choose her — not someone else — but her. That's kind of a big deal, considering there are 3.4 billion women (or thereabouts) on the planet. You chose *her* over all of them.

And she, of course, wasted no time sliding that costly piece of precious metal around her finger. Not just because it's beautiful and costly and precious — like her — but because it sings! It sings when she walks into the hair salon. It sings when she strolls into Starbucks. It sings when she hails a taxi, takes notes in class, or Skype's with a friend. It sings in every language, because its song is understood by every soul who's ever yearned for love and belonging: *"Someone chose me!"*

Something so dainty never broadcast a message so thunderous.

Your personal Instagram announcement probably said something clever like, "She said *Yes!*" or "Meet the future Mrs. So-and-So!" But what you really meant was, "Here's the one I've chosen!"

Her parents made it official with fancy invitations to a formal ceremony centered around sacred vows: "We're pleased to announce our precious daughter has been chosen for matrimony. Come meet the man who chose her." Stripped down, that's the essence of every wedding invitation.

It's also the lifeblood of every thriving marriage, found in three simple words:

Keep choosing her.

THERE'S NO PLACE LIKE HOME

OK, so the secret sauce isn't so secret. You certainly don't need the wizard's help, and quite frankly, you don't need mine. You already have enough brains, enough courage, and enough heart to build a world-class marriage. If Glinda the Good Witch[28] descended out of the sky right now, she'd smile and say in a brightly reassuring voice, "You've always had the power to understand your wife and make her happy, you just needed to learn it for yourself. Now close your eyes, tap your work boots (or wingtips) together three times, and think to yourself: *Keep choosing her … keep choosing her … keep choosing her … keep choosing her … keep choosing her …*"

Choosing her is the opposite of ignoring her, of neglecting her, of leaving her. And if your wife has ever been A-worded, building the keep-choosing-her habit is how you create a marriage she can heal and flourish in. It's also how you crush the head of the serpent.

Here's something I have all my clients do: First, find an endearing photo of your wife. Next, use a simple photo editing tool to add a thought bubble with three words inside:

Frame it and put it somewhere conspicuous. Make it your cell phone's lock screen. And remember, despite what the Propaganda Machine tells you:

Your wife isn't impossible to understand.

She's *not* an Advanced Biochemistry textbook.

She's a flashcard with *1+1* written on it.

The key to her heart — and to stratospheric sex — is actually quite simple:

Keep choosing her.

Now you know.

WAYS TO KEEP CHOOSING HER

- Give her a five-minute shoulder or foot massage
- Clean out her car
- Turn off SportsCenter and go to bed when she does (this one has a massive, tsunami-like ripple effect)
- Side with her during a family conflict
- Call in sick and spend the morning with her
- List the qualities that first attracted you to her and recite them at the dinner table
- Hold her when she's sad
- Plan a surprise party for her next birthday and have each guest prepare something meaningful to say. You go last
- Slow dance in public
- Comment on how beautiful she looks

- Buy her *a shared experience* — instead of *a thing*

- Hold her hand

- Practice being "strategically unavailable" when you're together (turn off your phone)

- Leave her a sticky note

- Open a life insurance policy

- Knock an item off her honey-do list without being asked

- Learn her love language (5lovelanguages.com)

- Take her out!

- Organize a weekly "business" meeting to discuss finances, priorities, calendars, the kids, date nights, weekend plans, chores, etc.

- Take her shopping for new clothes

- When in doubt, go after her

- Kiss her for 20 seconds (with no sexual overtones or innuendo)

- Compliment her: "I was just admiring how you … "

- Turn off the PS4 and help her with the kids

- Call to say "I love you," or to ask how her day is going (or both)

- Read her your wedding vows on your next date (or write new ones)

- Mail her a postcard from work

- Do something fun together!

- Give her the last scoop of ice cream

- Look at her like you did when you first met

- And *never* volunteer to sleep on the couch

Although your wife isn't a project, put a check mark next to each item upon its completion (and jot down a few ideas of your own). Reading over this list a few hundred times will inculcate your subconscious with the keep-choosing-her habit until it becomes second nature.

Eventually, she'll forget her heart was ever trampled on.

Romance Made Simple

For women, the best aphrodisiacs are words. The G-spot is in the ears. He who looks for it below there is wasting his time.

—ISABEL ALLENDE

Romance isn't the transcendent, hard-to-put-a-finger-on-it mystery we've made it out to be. Quite the contrary, it's stunningly simple. At its core, romance isn't flowers or fancy dinners. It's not candles or come-hither looks. It's not passion or poetry, bubble baths or biscotti. It's not even seduction or sex. The essence of romance is *attention*. And the language of romance is, "I'm thinking about you."

Simple, right?

"I'm thinking about you."

The verb tense *past continuous* also qualifies: "I *was* thinking about you."

- "I was thinking about you when I made this."
- "I was thinking about you when I wrote this."

- "I was thinking about you when I planned this."
- "I was thinking about you when I bought this."
- "I was thinking about you when I drew this."
- "I was thinking about you when I made a special trip to get this."
- "I was thinking about you when I composed this."
- "I was thinking about you when I painted this."
- "I was thinking about you when I built this."
- "I was thinking about you when I prepared this."

It's food and drink to a woman's soul — like red Twizzlers and apple martinis.

You see, it's not the *actual* gift you bought. The gift itself might be ugly in her estimation. It's what the gift represents: you were thinking about her. It's not the *actual* poem you wrote. The poem itself might be dreadful. It's what the poem represents: you were thinking about her. It's not the *actual* meal you prepared. The meal itself might be dry and overcooked. It's what the meal and the work that went into it represent: you were thinking about her. It's not the *actual* date you planned. You might discover shooting ranges aren't her thing. It's what the initiative and planning represent: you were thinking about her. That's not insignificant considering 50,000 to 70,000 images and ideas race through our minds every 24 hours.

It really *is* the thought that counts.

That's why sex without romance, over time, can be so detrimental to a woman's psyche. If romance says, "I'm thinking about you," sex without romance says, "I'm thinking about *me*." I'm amazed women stick around as long as they do, when the message we repeatedly send is, "I'm not into you, I'm into me."

ORAL SEX FOR SISSIES

Can giving your wife flowers be romantic? Of course. Particularly when it's for no good reason, other than to say, "I was thinking about you." So can leaving a handwritten note. Or any other simple gesture. I used to drop by the hair salon where my wife worked and leave a bottle of her favorite smoothie, *Mango Tango*. Simple, inexpensive, but unmistakable — "I was thinking about you." Early in our relationship, I sent her two or three postcards per week, even though we lived in the same city and eventually the same house. She saved every one. I looked through a pile of them yesterday. To show you how easy this is, and possibly to inspire you, here are a few of the poems, limericks, and odes I penned and snail-mailed to my wife:

> Your hair is red
> My hair is not
> Just a quick note
> In case you forgot
> I LOVE YOU
> [Pssst: they *always* forget.]

> You are the answer
> To all my heart's burning

Even now as I write
Every ounce of me's yearning

To be joined with the one
My soul craves to know
A business trip
Never went so slow

You are my leading lady
You are the momma who makes the drama of this life
worthwhile
Your smile reminds me I have so much to be grateful for
You will always be the color in my black and white world
Love, your leading man

Love you deeply
Love you dearly
Love you weekly
Love you yearly

Love you waking
Love you sleeping
Love you laughing
Love you weeping

Whether you're happy
Or whether you pout
I'm gonna love you
From here on out

Thinking of you through the day
I'm really just wanting to say
I love you so much
I wish I could touch
You in a biblical way

My love, if you're reading this postcard while I'm standing nearby:

1. Smile and walk swiftly in my direction
2. Jump into my arms, wrap your legs around me, and kiss me like you mean it.

P.S. If I'm not home yet, greet me at the door when I arrive and refer to step number two.

Trends come and go
Companies hire and fire
Fashions change
Markets fluctuate
Birds fly south
Friends move away…
I'm staying

Are there still only 24 hours in a day…
Or does time just *seem* to crawl when I'm not with you?

I love you when you ovulate
I love you when you don't
I love you when you smile at me
I love you when you won't

I love you when you stay up late
And kiss me on the lips
I love you when we're far apart
Or joining at the hips

What I'm trying hard to say
Through this simple rhyme
No matter what you've done or do
I love you all the time

If I had wings
I'd jump out of this 7th floor window
And fly to where you are

You are my beautiful and noble princess
Waiting in the dark tower
I am your brave and valiant warrior
Piercing the dragon's heart
Just a few more feet to the top of the tower
And you'll be in my arms…
For good

Reading through the thousands of lines I composed, I notice a recurring theme: "I'm not going anywhere. I'm not waiting for something better to come along. *You* are my one and only. There's nothing you can do to make me love you any more or any less. I love you. Period." And this was before I knew about the "A" word and my wife's repeated run-ins with it.

No wonder she saved each one.

POSTCARDS ARE KING

I recommend postcards over other writing forms for one simple reason: They yield the highest return on investment. Postcards get read over and over again. *And over.* Consider: Emails get pushed to the bottom of the inbox. Letters get stuffed back into envelopes. Texts get bumped off the screen and eventually disappear. Not postcards. They can be prominently pinned, taped, or attached to just about anything. They can be wedged, leaned, or displayed just about anywhere. Sticky notes and greeting cards are a close second.

"But Jeff, I'm not a writer."

That's complete bullcrap! Neither was I. My writing career began the moment I met the woman who stole my heart. If you love someone, you're a writer, you're a poet. And if you're a husband, it's part of your unwritten job description.

C'mon, how difficult is this:

> Your hair is red (or brown, or blond, or black)
> My hair is not
> Just a quick note
> In case you forgot
> I LOVE YOU

Anybody can do that! Just get started. You'll improve as you go. Buy a few postcards and keep them handy. Your prose needn't be lengthy or catchy. The British Invasion was launched with, "I wanna hold your hand." If you get stuck, steal a line or two from someone else. I did. I stole from John Lennon and T.S. Eliot and even Madonna once. It's legal. Trust me, your wife will be smitten either way.

She's *starving* for words.

THERE'S A PROSTITUTE IN ALL OF US

What if I told you there's a way to lower your wife's blood pressure by 10 points *and* upgrade your lovemaking to the first-class cabin for less than 95 cents a day?

Interested?

I'm guessing *Yes,* or maybe even *YES!* But if that's the case, why do so many of us drag our feet when it comes to getting a life insurance policy? Maybe it's the finger prick and urine sample. I know … you're wondering what life insurance has to do with sex and why I'm bringing it up in a chapter about romance. I'll get to that in a second. First, my story:

I got pricked two or three years into my marriage. My wife was pushing me to get pricked much sooner, but guys with cones on their heads shy away from sharp needles and responsibility. Plus, I was getting annoyed and slightly freaked out by her unflagging insistence. "Is there a contract on my head?! Does she *want* me to die?! Is money all she cares about?!"

No, Einstein. She expects *you* to care about *her.* She expects *you* to care about what happens to *her* if something tragic and unexpected were to happen. She expects *you* to have a life insurance policy in place so *she* and the kids will be OK.

That's why getting pricked is big time romantic. Because nothing says, "I'm thinking about you," quite like life insurance.

- "I've made sure you'll be provided for in case I'm gone."

- "You won't lose the house."

- "You won't have to downsize."

- "You can sleep better knowing you and the kids will be taken care of."

- "Nothing's more important to me."

Now you're speaking her language.

A TALE OF TWO PRICKS

Life insurance is the highest rung of the romance ladder. Higher than poems or postcards or proposing on the observation deck of the Empire State Building. Higher than scalp massages or caramel corn or sitting arm-in-arm on the veranda as the sun's last rays paint the sky. That's why postponing the prick is so detrimental to your sex life. I'm betting your dad didn't even mention it during his "birds and the bees" talk, but I've seen this play out in countless marriages. Putting off the prick causes more dissension and smothers more romantic fires than *The Big Three *combined*.

On the flip side, the advantages of acquiring life insurance are dramatic and immediate. In my home, the approval of my application for a one million dollar policy triggered a bull market upturn in both the frequency and intensity of our lovemaking.

Not bad for a small prick and 95 cents a day.

What men *think* women want is money; what women *actually* want is security. And long before they strive for financial security, they strive for relational security. A little girl doesn't dream of 401Ks and enough money in the bank for retirement. She dreams of a valiant man who'll fight for her heart and make her his priority.

Life insurance is a way to give your wife the whole enchilada: financial security *and* relational security.

So yes, this one time, go ahead and pay for sex.

You romantic, you.

*The Big Three:
1. Different Parenting Styles *(You let him get away with that?!)*

2. Different Thermostat-Setting Preferences *(An oven?! I'm freezing!)*

3. Different Interpretations of the Term "Five Minutes" *(I'll be ready in five minutes, I'll be home in five minutes, I was only gone for five minutes)*

Salvation Comes in a Tiffany Blue Bag

Deep in every heart slumbers a dream,
and the couturier knows it: Every woman is a princess.
—CHRISTIAN DIOR

A few words and phrases likely to unnerve even the most stalwart among us:

- *Accessorize*

- *This one's out of fashion*

- *I'm going shopping in the city tomorrow with the girls*

- *Three new outfits*

- *Prada*

- *Hand embroidered*

- *Matching handbag*

- *They were having a clearance sale*

- *I put it all on the card*

- *Update* and *wardrobe* in the same sentence

- *More closet space*

- *Michael Kors*

- *We came, we saw, we conquered!*

- *Diamond encrusted*

- *Real ostrich skin*

- *It's from Tiffany's*

In the early days of our marriage, I thought *The Shopping Network* was what my wife and her friends called themselves — their name on the street. I was mistaken, of course, it's a TV channel, but the label was fitting, nonetheless. These women controlled a large mall, fought rival housewife gangs for turf rights, and communicated via code words and hand signs in order to keep bloodhound husbands off their trail. They took shopping *very* seriously.

Us guys, not so much. We're utility shoppers. We shop when we absolutely have to, and not a minute before. Case in point: I'm sitting at my desk just before dawn, wearing the tartan plaid boxers I slept in. I may as well be naked though, because the fly portion of my underwear is torn wide open. The "new fly" extends from the waistband all the way through the crotch. What used to be a four-inch slit is now a gaping fourteen-inch hole, leaving me completely exposed in the front. You won't see me taking out the trash in these babies! I'm laughing because it just occurred to me that it hasn't been two weeks or two months since I accidentally put my foot through the fly instead of the right leg hole … it's been over two *years*. And you know what? I'll sleep in 'em for *another* two years as long as the waistband holds out.

Your wife is different, thank God, but you won't understand why unless I tell you the bigger story.

THE BIGGER STORY

Your pets aren't the only ones keeping your wife company while you're at the office and the munchkins are at school. She's watched over by an evil stepmother named *Housework*: a control freak who keeps her shackled to menial chores and takes great delight in seeing her suffer in obscurity. It's *Work! Work! Work!* from dawn til dusk. And much like Perrault's *Cinderella*[29], her only reprieve is a few quiet moments to herself each night inside a cold and barren bedroom, warmed occasionally by a stranger she calls *Husband*.

That's not all. Day in and day out, as your wife scours and scrubs, she's abused by two demented stepsisters: *You're fat!* and *You're ugly!* They mock her mercilessly, pointing out how ordinary and undesirable she is. When the day arrives that a handsome prince invites all the fair ladies in the land to a spectacular ball, planning to choose a wife from among them, the elder sister taunts:

> "You're an embarrassment! You can't go to the ball looking like *that*. You'd be a laughingstock! Besides, frumpy old maids aren't welcome. Here, catch this. It's a recent issue of *InStyle* magazine with Heidi Klum on the cover. Stay home and pine over pictures of elegant and beautiful women while we enjoy ourselves at the ball. Have fu'un … ha ha ha ha ha ha!"

And *Shopping?* You've probably guessed — *Shopping* is her fairy godmother. Her salvation. The one who promises:

> "I will transform you! From common to captivating, from dull to glamorous, from porridge to habanero! Let's start with a sexy new top, a smoldering shade of eye shadow, and that delicious pair of pumps you saw at Barney's last week. Just wait till the king's son gets an eyeful of *you*. He won't know what hit him! Your days of toiling in obscurity will be over!"

For most women, shopping isn't shopping, it's a stairway to heaven.

IF THE GLASS SLIPPER FITS

Most men, especially the ones with expensive hobbies, give their wives a hard time about shopping for themselves. This is a really bad idea.

- "Didn't you just go shopping five months ago?!"
- "What's the big occasion?!"
- "Don't you already have a black dress?"
- "It cost *how* much?!"
- "What's wrong with the one you have?!"

Nothing. Absolutely nothing is wrong with the one she has, Mr Left Brain. The one she has is perfectly fine. But she looks *stunning* in this one. The jaws of *The Shopping Network* dropped in unison when she sauntered out of the dressing room in it — just like in the original story, when the violins stopped playing and a hush came over the crowd as Cinderella made her grand entrance.

Your wife isn't acting irresponsibly. She's not trying to break the bank. She's trying to escape a life of forced servitude! She wants to look beautiful; she wants to *feel* beautiful. She wants to come home and twirl around the living room in her new black dress. She wants you to *see her,* and to like what you see. She wants *your* jaw to drop. She's crossing her fingers and hoping you take her to the ball, or the gallery opening, or the fancy new restaurant all her friends are talking about. She imagines walking in on your arm, enchanting every person in the room.

Tomorrow — there will be diapers to change and mouths to feed. But tonight, before the spell is broken, she wants to be your princess.

So, the next time she heads out the door to shop for new sandals or a new skirt, smile and ask, "Don't you need a new handbag, too?"

She just might pick up some lingerie while she's at it.

[**Note:** This chapter is full of obvious stereotypes. Your marriage might look very different. Maybe your wife works. Maybe she makes more than you. And maybe shopping isn't her escape of choice. Whatever the case, encourage her to pursue her passions outside of the home. If she has a favorite hobby, surprise her with lessons or an afternoon away from the kids to practice her craft. If she'd rather hike with her girlfriends than shop, take her to REI for a new pair of hiking shoes. She just might pick up a sexy new sports bra while she's at it.]

Honeymoon Sex Now

You'll be glad every night that you treated her right.[30]
—GEORGE THOROGOOD

"Why is honeymoon sex so amazing?"

I posed this question to dozens of married women. Their responses point overwhelmingly to one simple answer:

Honeymoon sex is amazing because our wives are *fully present*.

Guys don't get this because we're *always* fully present when it comes to sex. Let's face it, much of our conscious energy is directed toward the planning and execution of our next liaison. There's no way we're checking out during the act itself. We are in the moment! But women are a different story. Their minds are often elsewhere during sex.

The question on the table then is this: What is it about the honeymoon that helps women be fully present during sex? Is it the tropical climate? tanned bodies? white sand beaches? Should we *move* to Maui?

Here's my easy-to-remember "Honeymoon Sex Now" equation:

No Messes + No Stresses + No Guesses = Mind-Blowing Sex

Let's break that down.

No Messes

This is a big deal. *Someone else* made the bed. *Someone else* picked up the wet towels. *Someone else* washed the sheets. *Someone else* left the bathroom sparkling clean. What a load off her mind!

No Stresses

It's much more than the white sand beaches. It's no screaming kids. No lunches to pack. No errands to run. No bills to pay. No boss to please. No meals to prepare. No books to return. Just plenty of time to do whatever she wants: work out, sit by the pool, enjoy a good book, sip a frozen daiquiri, take a nap in the shade … as stress-free as stress-free can be.

And most likely, she was rockin' her honeymoon body, which means she felt really good about herself. She was unencumbered from the stress of wishing she looked trimmer and sexier for her dashing groom. That kind of burden can weigh heavily on a woman.

No Guesses

Studies show that the majority of married women go through life with a question mark emblazoned across their frontal lobe. It manifests as a recurring loop: "Does he still love me? Am I still attractive to him? Do I still capture his attention, or does he think about other women?" These questions typically don't show up until sometime *after* the honeymoon.

You can guess why. There was zero room for doubt during your excursion in paradise. She received your undivided attention. She wasn't competing with anything or anyone else. She was the center of your universe. And she *knew* it.

Of course she did. You weren't distracted. You weren't pulled in a dozen different directions. There were no deadlines or late nights at the office. Your entire world was reduced to you and her.

You were fully present.

Which helped *her* be fully present.

In the next chapter I'll teach you how to recreate the experience and have honeymoon-caliber sex in the comfort of your own home and yard.

FOR GREATER OOMPH

Read the companion post "The Oxymoron That Could Heal (And Even Save) Your Marriage" at wifemagnet.me.

Better Sex Guarantee #4
-Put Her First-

There is nothing quite as sexy as a man who loves his wife.
Every woman in the room wants to be her.

—AS SEEN ON PINTEREST

This one pays dividends like Procter & Gamble on steroids.

Ready?

Get rid of your car.

Well, not entirely. But downsize it. Trade in your SUV or luxury sedan for a used economy car. I know, I know, economy cars are boring as crap. But what's more important to you: a thrilling commute or a thrilling sex life?

Here's how this one small sacrifice will propel your lovemaking quotient from anemic to atomic. It's so simple, you'll wonder why you didn't think of it yourself. Use the $200–300 you save each month to do two of the most important (but overlooked) things a husband could *ever* do:

1. Treat your wife to a spa day (once a month)

2. Hire a housecleaning service (every two weeks)

Did you hear that thundering explosion? It's news of your decision breaking the sound barrier. Shock waves are being felt for miles in every direction. Social media is blowin' up. You think I'm exaggerating? Not even close. This is an undersell. You're about to go viral.

Run-of-the-mill husbands don't do this kind of thing. Heck, *great* ones don't. You'll be in a class all your own.

YOUR EXPANDING SOCIAL NETWORK

Once her girlfriends get wind of this, it's over. You'll never have to blow your own horn again. They will do it for you. And they'll do it unsolicited for the rest of your life. A volunteer fan club — *women you don't even know* — routinely reminding your wife how lucky she is to have a husband like you. It's free money in your pocket every month!

Conversations like this will be a regular occurrence:

> **Your Wife:** "Hi Susan, can you pick up my boys after school today and have them over for an hour or two until I get home?"
>
> **Her Friend:** "Of course, anytime. Running a few errands?"
>
> **Your Wife:** "No, I'll be at the spa enjoying a deep tissue

massage and lavender sea salt scrub."

Her Friend: "Ooo, must be nice. Sounds like someone's husband got a raise."

Your Wife: "No, but he did trade in his X5 for an Elantra, so I could have a spa day and hire a house cleaning service every month. Isn't he amazing?!"

Her Friend: *"Yes!* Where do I get one?!"

Little do your male friends know you're the one to blame for the dramatic decline in their approval ratings. But they'll find out soon enough. When they confront you angrily, just smile, hand them this book, and say, "It's all in here."

WHY IT WORKS

Your wife will look forward to her spa day for *weeks* ahead of time. She'll breathe easier just knowing it's on the calendar. [Sound of deep inhale and long exhale] "Ahhhhhh ... spa day's comin' ..." That's not all. She'll feel refreshed and invigorated for days afterward. I don't know if you're counting, but that's lots and lots of points for the home team, my friend.

Hiring a crew to clean the house means she'll have time for herself — to work out, go shopping, get her nails done, meet a friend for coffee — whatever fills her tank. Instead of feeling depleted at day's end, she'll feel replenished and renewed. Again, that bodes well for you.

Here's a sure-fire way to get more bang for your buck (no pun intended): Take your wife out for dinner on the same day your home gets vacuumed and mopped by a third party. She'll arrive at the restaurant already basking in the afterglow of knowing her house is sparkling clean and she didn't have to lift a finger. You have set the mood in spades.

If the weather's nice, sit on the patio. She'll want the whole town to see her out with her man. Pretend not to notice the confident, cavalier-esque way she smiles at female passersby. It's her way of saying, "Mmm-hmm. I'm the woman you heard about — the one whose husband traded in his car so she could have a spa day and hire a maid. I'd be jealous, too." Let her preen awhile. She deserves it. You are allowed, however, to notice and comment on how stunning, radiant, and ravishing she looks.

GET CREATIVE

"But Jeff, I don't have a luxury car."

No problem. What *do* you have? A gun collection? An expensive golfing habit? What about that season ticket money? The choice is yours: Keep your guns and have unenthused sex with your wife once a quarter, or live with a woman who feels cherished and enjoys making love to her husband on a regular basis.

Start out smaller if money is an issue. What if you treated her to a spa day every other month and scheduled a cleaning service in 3–4 week intervals instead? Anyone can make that happen. It means she's getting a full-body massage six more times than she did last year. It means *someone else* is doing all the heavy lifting — the household stuff she hates — like cleaning the tub, mopping floors, and scrubbing toilets. And you? You're still in better-sex heaven.

HOW TO HANDLE SARCASM FROM CLUELESS MEN

Respond to sarcasm from clueless members of the male species by being straightforward and honest. Not too honest, though. They're already beaten down. Be gentle. Remember, they're our brothers, and we *all* flew the clueless flag longer than we'd care to admit.

> **Clueless Friend:** "What's with the lame set of wheels? Did you forget where your X5 was parked? Ha ha ha."
>
> **You:** "No, I traded it in. I'm using the extra money to hire a house cleaner and treat my wife to a spa day every month. I read it radically improves your sex life."
>
> **Clueless Friend:** "How's it working?"
>
> **You:** "Better than I ever imagined. My wife is like an animal again."
>
> **Clueless Friend:** "Damn."
>
> **You:** "I know."

As word spreads (and it will), you might consider getting into the used car business.

THE TREASURE PRINCIPLE

Everything I've shared in this chapter is true. I haven't embellished a single thing. This one small sacrifice *will* propel you to hero status at home and in your community. It *will* lead to mind-blowing sex. But I'd be less than honest if I didn't say what I'm about to say:

The biggest change won't take place in your bedroom.

It will take place in *you*.

There's a timeless spiritual principle that says, "Where your treasure is, there your heart will be also."[31] In other words, whatever you invest in, your heart will grow more fond of — more attached to.

We've all seen this.

What happens to the guy who spends two grand on a set of golf clubs? He stares at them. He cleans them. He covers and protects them. He thinks about them while he's at work. He brings friends over so he can show off his new driver. He carries his putter around the house. His pitching wedge in the yard. He practices more. He plays more. He plays *better*. He is a study in preoccupation.

This same is true in marriage.

When you give up something you love, in order to cherish and esteem your wife — by downsizing your car, or selling those clubs, or watching the Cowboys at home instead of the 50 yard line — something mystical and profound happens:

Your heart grows more fond of — more attached to — *her*.

You think about her more often. You wonder how her day is going. You check in more than you used to. You miss those eyes. That smile. That hair. Instead of rushing out the door in the morning, you hold her a little longer. Squeeze her a little tighter. You feel blessed to be her husband. You care deeply about her well-being. You make sure your life insurance policy is up to date. You fantasize Mortal Kombat-style about what you would do to the person who lays a finger on her. You want to be her hero.

Do you see what's happened?

Better sex is just icing on the cake.

You've become a better husband. You've become a better *man*.

And every time you climb into your economy car without climate control or a rearview camera, it's a tangible reminder you have something much more valuable than a stupid luxury car. You have a wife who trusts you, respects you, and believes in you.

You can't put a price tag on that.

This Chapter Will Save You *Lots* of Time

The short-term pain of accepting a truth is much better than the long-term pain of believing an illusion.

−LILKA

I hate to do this because it cheapens the rest of the book, but I'm offering you a shortcut, one that will fast-track you to the front of the line. One that will give you instant access to all the sex you could possibly imagine. One that will allow you to bypass everything we've talked about so far — all the hard work, all the commitment, all the sacrifice — *and still get the girl.*

First, I need your word you'll keep this between us. Don't share what I'm about to reveal with the guys who haven't read this far. And get ready to toss this useless piece of crap in the trash. You won't be needing it.

Here it is — the tested and proven shortcut that makes the rest of this book obsolete — two words:

Use porn.

Yes, use porn. It will make you a better man, give you what you want, and even resolve your intimacy issues. Plus, it's quick and easy.

All of that is true, of course, except for the part about making you a better man, giving you what you want, and resolving your intimacy issues.

AN INCONVENIENT TRUTH

I recently perused the really cool website of an organization that relies on science and fact, not morality, to educate people about the harmful effects of pornography. It was launched by a handful of college students out of Utah. I love their approach, I dig what they do, I already mentioned the website, but it's their name that caught my attention: *Fight the New Drug.*

Porn, a drug? I realize it can be addictive for some, but ... *a drug?* Really, young hipsters, I think you're overreaching. Drugs are what we use to relieve stress. Or numb our pain. Or escape a reality we feel powerless to change. Drugs are how we create a fantasy world where nothing is required of us. Or demanded of us. Where everything is just the way we ... whoops, never mind.

Our relationship with porn might change if we viewed it the way we view heroin. Or Celebrex. At least prescription drug companies are required by law to present the benefits and risks of their products "in a balanced fashion." And ya gotta tip your hat to 'em, because they do it spectacularly well. Their TV advertisements depict attractive and energetic people smiling, horseplaying, and sharing tender moments. Their homes are modern and immaculately kept. The scenes are so magical (even the teenagers are smiling), you'll hardly notice when the soothing voiceover transitions from the drug's benefits to risks. I transcribed this one word-for-word from an actual commercial:

> This medication may cause serious allergic reactions or suicidal thoughts or actions. Tell your doctor right away if you have these: new or worsening depression, unusual changes in mood or behavior, or swelling of the face, mouth, lips, gums, tongue, throat, or neck; trouble breathing, rash, hives, blisters, muscle pain with fever, tired feeling, or blurry vision. Common side effects are dizziness, sleepiness, weight gain, and swelling of the hands, legs, and feet.

May cause … *suicidal actions?! Are they serious?!* You mean like walking in front of a train or putting a gun in my mouth? If only the porn industry was forced to be this honest. Imagine if every trip down Porn Lane was pre-empted with:

> What you're about to view is more potent than high-grade heroin and faster in its onset of action. It will hijack your brain's reward center, carving new and dangerous neural pathways, which, in turn, will render you incapable of forming close and satisfying relationships. In lieu of a happy ending, you'll be left feeling even more frustrated, hollow, and unfulfilled.

> Evidence suggests porn will not solve your problems at home, but likely exacerbate them and create new

ones. Pornographic use is shown to increase marital tension and discord, erode trust, destroy intimacy, and heighten feelings of resentment. Even a strong marriage cannot compete with the unnatural and artificial levels of chemical excitement porn offers. Men who indulge rate themselves as less in love with their partner, less attracted to their partner, less satisfied with their partner, and more critical of their partner's appearance. They also cite greater frequency of erectile dysfunction, premature ejaculation, and involuntary outbursts of road rage. Spouses report feelings of loss, betrayal, mistrust, devastation, and anger. Many exhibit symptoms of anxiety and depression, with an increase in suicidal thoughts and actions.

Porn, like all medications, carries some risk of dependency. Get help right away if you have these: new or worsening insecurity, unusual changes in sexual preferences, emotional detachment, lack of empathy toward your spouse, sleeplessness, chronic self-loathing, unrealistic expectations in marriage, or a tendency to objectify women. Common side effects include denial, self-centeredness, isolation, shorter attention span, decreased productivity, and carpal tunnel syndrome. Studies show that married men who look at porn are more likely to cheat on their wives, visit prostitutes, confuse sex with love, and trade time with their children for time alone in a dark room. In some cases, repeated exposure to pornography leads to sexual compulsion, sexual addiction, sexual assault, divorce, loss of employment, and soullessness.

Individual results may vary.

The world you're about to enter isn't real. It erroneously depicts the fairer sex as subordinate and less-than-human, nothing more than objects to be used and consumed. The women on your screen are actresses—wind-up dolls surgically enhanced, airbrushed, and photoshopped for your sexual pleasure. They don't actually *enjoy* being exploited, manhandled, abused, hit, yelled at, humiliated, and otherwise mistreated. It's make-believe. A distortion. What you *will* see in this fictional online world are smiling and seductive faces. What you *won't* see are the grimaces, STDs, intestinal parasites, cervical cancer, bruises, torn skin, mounds of bloody tissues, anal and vaginal surgical repairs, unwanted pregnancies, abortions, or the teenage girl crying alone off camera. The majority of these "stars" were sexually abused as children. A handful were lured into porn under false pretenses and subsequently kidnapped, threatened, beaten, and raped in order to crush their spirits. (Some of the material you're about to view contains actual footage of their indoctrination.) We coerce and even force our actresses to do things that are dehumanizing. It's the reason 75% of them numb themselves with drugs or alcohol prior to filming.

Enjoy!

And that's the sanitized version.

BIGGER AND BETTER

I like looking at pictures of naked women (hardly a groundbreaking admission), but I'd much rather get my hands on a real one. It's the reason I stay away from porn. It's not because I'm a saint, it's because I've read the fine print.

Porn is a colossal rip-off.

It's also a powerful and addictive drug, one that will grind *you* to powder. If porn has been one-upping you lately, I've got some really good news:

1. You're not alone

2. Help is just a mouse-click away

You can find it at *XXXChurch.com. I've known the staff up close for nine years, and they're some of the most caring, down-to-earth, gracious people I know. Through workshops, blogs, software, videos, and peer support, they help ordinary Joes (and Josephines) live bigger lives.

Life is better without porn.

Marriage is better without porn.

Sex is better without porn.

You're better without porn.

*10% of this book's proceeds support the work of XXXChurch (referenced above) and the International Justice Mission — a human rights agency that rescues women and children from slavery, sex trafficking, and forced prostitution. IJM also provides aftercare to victims and works with the appropriate agencies to prosecute their abusers.

I *highly* recommend both of these world-class organizations.

Better Sex Guarantee #5
-Show Appreciation-

*Women have that weird way of trying to be feminist.
You know, like, "Hear me roar." But what they really want
is a man to open the door for them.*

−LESLIE BIBB

Are you married to a stay-at-home mom? It's easy to forget she does a crap-load of housework every single day. (Much of it involves *actual* loads of crap.) Making breakfast, doing dishes, getting kids ready for school, packing lunches, changing diapers, shopping for groceries, vacuuming dog hair, chopping vegetables, sweeping the floor, making smoothies, folding laundry, putting things away, cleaning mirrors, running errands, preparing healthy snacks, wiping up spills, driving kids all over creation, getting dinner ready, scrubbing pans, taking out the trash, picking up toys, helping with homework, brushing, bathing…you get the idea. It never ends.

And because so much of what she does is routine, we come and go and barely notice. Even worse, some of us consistently overlook the things our wives get done around the house, and focus instead on the things that *don't* get done. Most of the women I speak with feel under-appreciated and even taken for granted. And we wonder why they're less than eager in the bedroom. William James, the 19th century father of American psychology, asserted, "The deepest craving of human nature is the need to be appreciated."

Bottom line? Gratitude goes a long way. "Thank you" goes a long way. But there are different ways to say it.

Join me at the dinner table.

Level 1

Without uttering a word of appreciation for the meal she cooked, you excuse yourself to take a phone call and don't return to the table.

If I were your wife, I wouldn't have sex with you either! It could land her in jail. Intimate relations with the dead is called necrophilia and is currently illegal in 28 states.

Level 2

"Thanks for dinner, babe, it was delicious."

One word: lame.

"Lame?! But I meant it."

Oh, it might be a sincere comment, but it won't even register with your wife. Woman are verbal creatures, remember. A broad comment like this, no matter how sincere, will go in one ear and out the other. A few days from now she'll be saying things like, "You don't appreciate anything I do! I cook delicious meals for you all the time, and you never even thank me."

You know I'm right.

Level 3

"Thanks for dinner, babe, it was delicious. I love what you did with the potatoes!"

Good, you're paying attention. Complimenting her about something specific won't have her jumping out of her chair, but at least it will register.

Level 4

"Thanks for dinner, babe, it was delicious. I love what you did with the potatoes! Is that a new recipe?"

Ahhhh, now we're talking! You've done much more than pay her a specific compliment — you've engaged her! She feels noticed. She feels appreciated. She feels loved. It's all about relationship, after all, and now you're r-e-l-a-t-i-n-g with her. Smiling, listening, making eye contact, reaching for her hand. Look at you go! A few more trips like this around the block, and the training wheels can come off.

Level 5

As the conversation outlined above draws to a close, begin clearing the table and let her know you'll take care of the dishes.

"I've got this, babe. You do SO MUCH around here. Why don't you relax and unwind. Go do something for *you*."

Don't wait for her to respond or fall prostrate at your feet, just act like this is normal, everyday behavior for you. Depending on who's in the room, she just might rip your clothes off then and there.

Hopefully you're not holding a stack of fine china.

Why She Nags

I date this girl for two years — and then the nagging starts:
"I wanna know your name."

−MIKE BINDER

Wedding vows, much like the women we love, come in all shapes and sizes. Although varied, there's a common theme running through each one. I'd sum it up like this: "I will never leave your side. I will love you and fight for you. In good times and in bad. When I feel like it and when I don't. No matter what we face, we'll face it together. Only death could take me away from you."

And you know what? Any guy worth his salt meant every word on his wedding day. Some of us took a little longer getting to the altar than others, but once there, we took our commitment and our vows *very* seriously. Most of the men I know intend to stick by the women they love come hell or high water.

"But what if she contracts a debilitating disease?"
Not gonna scare me away!

"What about a disfiguring accident?"
I can handle it!

"A double mastectomy?"
If Brad did it, so can I!

"A controlling and suffocating mother-in-law?"
No problemo!

"A little nagging?"

"I said, a little nagging?"

"Hello?"

There's only one thing that compels a man to run away from the same woman he once ran toward — nagging. King Solomon, considered one of the wisest men who ever lived, passed this insightful tidbit to his sons:

> "Better to live out in the desert than with a nagging, complaining wife."[32]

Amen! I'll take solitude with the requisite blistering sun, scorpions, and risk of death by dehydration over the company of a nagging woman *any* day. 126 degrees with peace and quiet? Ahhhh, feels like the first day of spring!

Nagging is hard to be around. Many of the men I coach use massive amounts of creative energy (they lie) in order to avoid the women they love. Ironically, it's equal to the massive amounts of creative energy they employed in years past to win the hearts of the very same women.

Husband: "Hi honey, I can't leave the office until I finish this project. I'll be home late, unfortunately."

Wife: "I can't stand that boss of yours! He always does this to you."

Husband: "I know, it really sucks."

Husband: "Babe, I've gotta run! I have a softball game tonight."

Wife: "A softball game?! It's raining cats and dogs!"

Husband: "I know. We'll just have to wait it out. Hopefully I'll be home in a few hours."

Husband: "I'm helping Mike move this Saturday. I'll be gone most of the day."

Wife: "Didn't he just move a few months ago?"

Husband: "Yeah, but he hates the kitchen wallpaper in his new place."

Wife: "Kitchen wallpaper?! Why doesn't he just change it?!"

Husband: "Well, it's not just that. The trash pick-up at his old place was every Tuesday, but it's every Monday at his new place. He's having trouble adjusting and keeps putting his garbage out a day late, so it sits and sits, and now it's piling up everywhere, so he's moving to a zone in the city where the trash gets picked up on Tuesdays again. Crazy, right? You know Mike …"

Building a second home in the desert can be tricky.

Plus, it's tiring. And dishonest. And weak. Let's not leave out ineffective. Face it, when has dodging and avoiding her made things better? Or brought an end to her nagging? Or led to great sex?

Maybe we're missing something.

Here's the million-dollar-better-sex question: What if nagging isn't part of her DNA, but merely a *symptom* of something deeper?

- Hint #1: It always is
- Hint #2: Learning Hint #1 will change your marriage and sex life forever

Beneath that beautiful exterior of hers simmers a scorned and angry woman. She's hurt. She's fed up. She's tired of feeling neglected and pushed to the side. She's tired of having to fight for the scraps from your table. She wishes you showed more interest in her. It wounds her that you don't.

I didn't understand this until it was too late.

Nagging is how women defend themselves. Words are their strength! What women lack in brawn, they more than make up for in linguistic prowess.

"Oh, yeah? You're gonna dismiss me by working late every night?! By spending Saturday in front of the TV?! Watch me dismiss *you* with a roll of the eyes or a subtle put-down. Watch me dismiss *you* as I nag and pester you about every stupid little thing. I'll make your life miserable, you bastard!"

Each critical and fault-finding word is her version of a persistent jab. *Jab. Jab. Jab. Jab.* Withholding sex is her right-hand cross. *BAM.* And make no mistake about it: Her goal is to knock you on your ass. To hit you so hard you'll think twice about neglecting her again.

Isn't it what we teach our kids? "Don't ever be a bully, but if someone hits you, stand up for yourself and hit them back." Your wife must have overheard the conversation, because that's exactly what's going in your marriage. She's tired of being your punching bag. She's standing up for herself and hitting you back.

In a tender and honest moment once, my wife admitted she hated who she was when she nagged me. Don't think your wife feels any different. She hates nagging you and chasing you around.

She'd much rather have *you* chasing her again.

FOR GREATER OOMPH

Read the companion post "Her Half-Assed Effort Detector (And its Origin)" at wifemagnet.me.

Boy, You're Gonna Carry That Weight a Long Time

In the arithmetic of love, one plus one equals everything,
and two minus one equals nothing.

—MIGNON MCLAUGHLIN

Our final approach begins with an excerpt from an ancient book of wisdom. It's not the kind of advice you hear every day:

"Better to spend your time at funerals than at parties."[33]

Mic drop.

Huh?!

"I got my schwerve on at Murphy's Funeral Home this weekend! It was outta control!" said no one, ever. Funerals are somber. *And quiet.* Talk above a whisper and you'll be escorted out. Then there's the dreaded handshake. The one with the person who just lost their parent or child or spouse:

"Hi, I barely know you, but let me shake your hand and

offer my condolences and try to sound sincere when I say exactly what all 243 people ahead of me said: *I'm sorry for your loss.* There, I hope that softens the blow."

I mean, I know it helps because I've been the hand-shakee, but have you ever felt more uncomfortable? More inadequate? And yet the writer of Ecclesiastes says we're better off spending Saturday afternoon at the local mortuary than at the poolside tiki bar.

What's up with that?!

Here's my best guess: While parties tend to dull our higher senses, funerals sharpen them. The specter of death grabs our attention like nothing else. Whether it's kneeling before a casket or sitting in a doctor's office holding your loved one's hand and hearing the words, "three to six months," we're reminded just how fragile and fleeting — *how precious* — life is. Moments like these force us to confront the truth we'd all much rather avoid:

We're going to die. Fairly soon. And no one gets a do-over.

Suddenly, our priorities become crystal clear. We gain a new and profound awareness of what matters … and what doesn't. We're the most lucid we've been in a long time.

Death is a powerful motivator.

Now that our wheels have touched down, join me in the funeral parlor also known as divorce court.

THE DAY THE MUSIC DIED

Our divorce was finalized in a New Jersey courtroom on January 28, 2014. Nothing could have ever prepared me for the moment I stood with my hand on a Bible in a room full of strangers, just a few feet away from the woman I dreamed of growing old with, as a judge pronounced the dissolution of our union. Hot tears streamed silently down my face as I stared straight ahead and tried not to look pathetic. I held it together long enough to pick up my copy of the divorce decree, exit the courthouse, and walk to my car. Once inside, I exploded with emotion. Time was suspended as I death-gripped the steering wheel and screamed myself hoarse. It felt like a bad dream I'd never wake up from.

Fortunately, I had time to compose myself before picking up my son from school. I smiled at him as he ducked his head into the front passenger's seat. I'll never forget the look on his face as he studied mine, searching for a clue as to how my court date went. Finding none, he asked:

"Did mom change her mind?"

"No, son. She didn't. Our divorce was finalized a few hours ago."

I changed the subject and asked him about his day, but his mind was elsewhere. I had no idea that my son — in his little 12-year-old heart, right up to the very end — held out hope his parents would get back together and that we'd be a family again. Clueless dad and heartbroken son pulled into the driveway a few minutes later.

I resumed folding laundry in my bedroom when I heard a shriek so loud and so unusual, for a brief moment I thought a wild animal had gotten into our home. My heart racing, I ran into the hallway to find my son hunched over in defeat, wailing uncontrollably. The moment he secretly hoped would never arrive had come crashing down upon his head. I fell to my knees and held him as he sobbed on my shoulder. All I could do was add my tears to his and whisper, "I'm sorry. Daddy is *so* sorry."

THE GONE FOR GOOD, THE BAD, AND THE UGLY

In no particular order, here's a handful of words and phrases commonly associated with divorce:

> grief, anguish, sorrow, depression, emotional trauma, betrayal, infidelity, heartbreak, anger, guilt, regret, bitterness, resentment, blame, finger-pointing, revenge, litigation, custody battle, smear campaign, hostility, restraining order, frozen bank accounts, attorney fees, massive financial toll, decreased standard of living, stress, anxiety, adrenal fatigue, energy depletion, sleepless nights, long-term negative health consequences, reduced life expectancy, distress, eating disorder, substance abuse, rejection, insecurity, low self-esteem, choosing sides, child support, visitation rights, "See you in two weeks," sporadic contact, strained relationship, frustration, disappointment, divided loyalties, single parenthood, dissolved friendships, social withdrawal, isolation, loss of intimacy, and feelings of failure.

Whoops, I almost left one out: irreconcilable differences.

HERE COMES THE SUN

I have a message for the senior citizens reading this book:

"Time is short."

I have a message for the twenty-somethings reading this book:

"Time is short."

I could have done something to prevent the collapse of my marriage, but I was weak and shallow and full of pride. I was surrounded by other coneheads. Regrettably, my opportunity has passed.

Yours hasn't.

What Do You Want?

*The greater danger for most of us lies not in setting our aim too high
and falling short, but in setting our aim too low and achieving our mark.*

—MICHELANGELO BUONARROTI

This is your "red pill or blue pill" moment of truth.

Close this book right now and the story ends. I'll refund your
money and forget we ever spoke. You can go back to sleeping on
the couch and being a cog in the machine.

Or ... decide to be the flame that sparks a revolution in your
marriage.

The choice is yours.

FIELD OF DREAMS

Drive north on the 101 Freeway out of Los Angeles and the scenery
changes quite dramatically. As you descend the Conejo Grade to
the coastal plain below, jagged peaks, canyons, and dusty trails are
replaced by verdant fields and migrant workers in wide-brimmed
straw hats. Strawberries, raspberries, lima beans, tomatoes, and

peppers ... as far as the eye can see.

Now, look at your marriage.

That's your field.

And just like the produce fields bordering the 101, your marriage didn't get this way by accident, and it didn't get this way overnight. It's showing you *exactly* what you've planted over the past few years. Please, let me save you some heartache, if you don't like what's growing in your field, don't go shopping for a new piece of ... land. In a few seasons, it will look just like the one you're staring at now.

No, if you want a different harvest, *begin planting different seeds.*

Today.

It's that simple.

Your marriage won't bloom immediately, of course. It might be months before the first tiny sprouts appear. But the seeds you plant today — by inviting feedback, by gathering your band of brothers, by opening slammed doors — *will grow* if you keep watering them. As sure as day and night and the turning of the earth.

JUST A GIRL

For weeks I wrestled over how to close this book. I pinned that demon to the mat the night I sat in our living room and watched *Notting Hill* with my son. If you haven't seen the movie, Julia Roberts plays Anna Scott, an even-more-famous-than-Julia-

Roberts American actress who's on location in London. Between takes, Anna walks into a tiny corner bookstore owned by William Thacker (Hugh Grant) — a divorced, unlucky-in-love, really nice guy. A whirlwind romance ensues, followed by a series of mishaps and the untimely appearance of Anna's on-again-off-again deadbeat boyfriend. Crushed and kicked to the curb, William licks his wounds and returns to his humdrum life.

Fast forward a year or so. A penitent Anna shows up in his bookstore unannounced, hoping to pick up where they left off. William refuses to budge — citing her fame, their polar-opposite lifestyles, and the likelihood of his heart being broken again. Swallowing her pride, a teary-eyed Anna braves this quintessential line:

> "The fame thing isn't really *real*, you know. And don't forget, I'm … I'm also just a girl … standing in front of a boy … asking him to love her."[34]

Your wife may nag you from time to time, but she's not a nag. She may act bitchy with the best of them, but she's not a bitch. She may rage and seethe and foam at the mouth, but she's not a lunatic. I'm guessing she's used her tongue to wound and emasculate you more than once, but she's not a cold-hearted assassin. Peel back the layers of hurt and misunderstanding …

… and she's just a girl, standing in front of a boy, asking him to love her.

The ball is in your court.

It's *always* in your court.

How to Stay in Beast Mode

In any given moment, we have two options:
step forward into growth or step backward into safety.
—ABRAHAM MASLOW

First, let me congratulate you. You did it! A lot of guys won't crack open a book to save their lives. An even smaller percentage are willing to read one about ruh … ruh … ruh-lay … relationships. You're among the world's elite now!

Let me also acknowledge what you figured out many chapters ago: This book isn't about sex. It's not even about winning her heart back. It's about getting *your* heart back! It's about waking up. And getting off the hamster wheel. And refusing to make excuses. It's about courage and valor and slaying the dragon. It's about building an unbreakable bond with the woman you chose to share your life with. Yes, you could say I tricked you, or you could say, "Just a spoonful of sugar helps the medicine go down."[35]

In the most *delightful* way.[36]

A BEGINNING, NOT AN ENDING

In my experience, most men have marriages that can only be described as "eh." So-so. Not *boo-yah,* not train wreck, just … "eh." Stuck in the mediocre middle.

Here's the head-scratcher: Like you, these men aren't jerks — most of them are *really* good guys. *Then why?!* Why has the fire gone out? Why are some — unbeknownst to them — even headed for divorce?

The answer is simple:

For most husbands — even the good ones — their marriages live in the *back* of their brains. Behind work and paying bills and trying to eat right and squeezing in a workout. W-a-a-a-y back there. That was my story. I wasn't a terrible person, but my mind wasn't on my marriage. It was on other things.

It's probably your story, too.

Today, your relationship with your wife is in the *front* of your brain where it belongs. Books like mine will do that. But over the ensuing weeks, your marriage, like a glacier, will slowly retreat to the back of your skull and settle into its former home. Sadly, most of the ground you've gained will be lost.

But what if there was a way to *keep* your marriage front and center? Keep you sharp. Keep you in beast mode.

I have really good news — now there is!

Welcome to my **Inner Circle**.

It's a private group for husbands who want my book to be a beginning, not an ending. Members receive new content from me every week in the form of videos and podcasts — including exclusive interviews with married women, divorced women, marriage counselors, and relationship gurus. They also enjoy direct access to me through a private Facebook group and live monthly masterminds. Most importantly, members of my **Inner Circle** are never alone. They're part of a brotherhood — a strong and supportive community of like-minded men.

Pardon the pun, but if you're determined to *stay* on this path and build a world-class marriage, it's a no-brainer! And the one-time "Founding Member" price of only $10 a month means it's the most intelligent and rewarding investment you'll ever make.

What Now? Visit wifemagnet.me/innercircle for your 30-day, risk-free trial. Or simply text me at (818) 209-6294.

Bringing sexy back has never been easier.

THE ONE PERCENT

For a moment, imagine you're inside a football stadium, down on the turf. You're standing shoulder to shoulder with 99 other men spanning the entire length of the field, goal line to goal line. Can you see it? I don't know what kind of physical shape you're in, but odds are you wouldn't be the strongest or fastest of the bunch. You would, however, dominate a much more important category: husbands whose wives think they hung the moon. I might be projecting a few months ahead, but it's true. You now know more about women and how they're wired than 99% of all men on the planet.

So?

So, this world needs you. Other men need you! Someone you know is stuck — *right now* — and has no idea how to fix his marriage. Who is it? Are you picturing a face? Buy him a copy of this book. Meet him for coffee or beer once a week. Listen. Be a sounding board. Encourage his newfound awareness. Don't keep your epiphanies to yourself, pay them forward! This is *your* story now. Keep the conversation going.

And remember to tell him, "No matter how bad things are right now, you're only one or two *Aha!* moments away from having steamy sex with your wife again. I couldn't be more serious."

–Jeff

BEFORE YOU GO ...

Would you do me one small favor?

If you enjoyed this book or found it helpful, would you leave a brief review on its Amazon page? Short and simple is fine. Your small investment will help extend my book's reach and bring hope and healing to more families!

Thank you.

FOR THOSE IN CRISIS » PRIVATE COACHING

Your future is already written. It's called your default future. It's where you'll end up if nothing changes. Ask yourself, *"What will my life be like a year from now — five years from now — if nothing changes?"* Coaching creates change. It creates ripples that reach into your future and rewrite it.

I'm all about one thing: *your transformation*. I don't do Band-Aids or quick fixes, but if you're ready to evolve — to move your marriage from cold-and-distant to close-and-intimate — I'm your guy.

Interested? Reserve your free private consultation. No strings, no gimmicks, nothing salesy. You hate that crap and so do I. Let's talk a few times to see if we're a good fit. Reach out to me below.

CONNECT WITH ME

It's a privilege to meet one of my readers. Do you have a question, comment, or just want to say hi? I'd love to hear from you! Call or text me at (818) 209-6294. Yes, it's my real cell phone number. You can also reach me via:

Email   jeff@wifemagnet.me

Facebook   facebook.com/wifemagnet

Instagram   instagram.com/jeffborkoski

P.S. *Don't lose momentum! Stay in beast mode!* Come join us at wifemagnet.me/innercircle. See you on the inside!

To My Scapegoat

You did the unthinkable — taking my place on a cross of shame. Words fall short. You have removed the sting of my failures.

> Who loved me through my rebel way
> Who chose to carry all my shame
> Who stands for all with arms stretched wide
> My King forever, Jesus Christ.[37]

To True Life Church (New Jersey)
and The Metro District of The C&MA

I'll never understand how people go through crisis without a community like this one around them. Not a day went by without someone calling, popping in, or leaving a meal outside the door. Your love and prayers sustained us. Thank you for giving me the time and resources I needed to heal and get my mojo back.

Notes

1. Tom Scholz. "More Than a Feeling." Boston. Vinyl. Epic Records, 1976.

2. John Pop. "The Bad Touch." Hooray for Boobies. CD. Geffen Records, 1999.

3. *Spider-Man*. Written by Stan Lee (comic book), Steve Ditko (comic book), and David Koepp (screenplay). Directed by Sam Raimi. Performances by Tobey Maguire, Kirsten Dunst, and Willem Dafoe. Columbia Pictures, 2002. DVD.

4. Darren Hardy. *The Compound Effect* (Vanguard Press, 2012).

5. Jeff Olson. *The Slight Edge* (Momentum Media, 2005), 27.

6. Ibid, 28.

7. Alex Ikonn. *The Five-Minute Journal* (Intelligent Change, 2013).

8. Proverbs 17:17 (RSV) — Taken from the Revised Standard Version of the Bible, copyright © 1946, 1952, and 1971 the Division of Christian Education of the National Council of the Churches of Christ in the United States of America. Used by permission. All rights reserved.

9. Ecclesiastes 4:12 (NLT) — Scripture taken from the Holy Bible, New Living Translation, copyright © 1996, 2004, 2007 by Tyndale House Foundation. Used by permission of Tyndale House Publishers, Inc., Carol Stream, Illinois 60188. All rights reserved.

10. John Lee Dumas. "Episode 900: Jack Canfield shares success principles and his worst entrepreneurial moment." Audio blog post. John Lee Dumas Chats with Jack Canfield. Entrepreneur On Fire. Web. April 9, 2015.

11. Ibid.

12. Ibid.

13. Ibid.

14. Ibid.

15. Casey Caston. "30 Questions to Ask Your Wife." Blog post. Marriage 365. April 4, 2016.

16. Ibid.

17. "10 Questions to Ask Your Wife Every Year." Blog post. All Pro Dad. Family First.

18. Ibid.

19. Ibid.

20. Matthew 5:25-26 (EXB) — Scripture taken from The Expanded Bible. Copyright © 2011 by Thomas Nelson. Used by permission. All rights reserved.

21. Francis Frangipane. *The Three Battlegrounds* (Arrow Publications, 2002), 18-22.

22. Paul Simon. "The Sound of Silence." Wednesday Morning, 3 A.M. Vinyl. Columbia Records, 1964.

23. Ibid.

24. *Taken.* Written by Luc Besson and Robert Mark Kamen. Directed by Pierre Morel. Performances by Liam Neeson, Famke Janssen, and Maggie Grace. 20th Century Fox, 2008. DVD.

25. Sheryl Crow, Bill Bottrell, Kevin Gilbert, Brian MacLeod, David Ricketts, and David Baerwald. "Strong Enough." Tuesday Night Music Club. Vinyl. A&M Records, 1993.

26. Shania Twain and R.J. Lange. Copyright © 1997 Loon Echo, Inc. and Out Of Pocket Productions Ltd. All rights for Loon Echo, Inc. controlled and administered by Songs of Universal, Inc. All rights for Out Of Pocket Productions Ltd. in the U.S. and Canada

controlled and administered by Universal-Polygram International Publishing, Inc. All rights reserved. Used by permission. Reprinted by permission of Hal Leonard LLC.

27. John Eldredge. *Wild at Heart* (Thomas Nelson, 2001), 17, italics in original.

28. *The Wizard of Oz.* Written by L. Frank Baum (book), Noel Langley (adaptation & screenplay), Florence Ryerson (screenplay), and Edgar Allan Woolf (screenplay). Directed by Victor Fleming. Performances by Judy Garland, Frank Morgan, and Margaret Hamilton. MGM, 1939.

29. Charles Perrault. "Cinderella," in Histoires ou contes du temps passé (Paris, 1697).

30. Roy Head and Gene Kurtz. "Treat Her Right." Born to Be Bad. Vinyl. EMI Records, 1988.

31. Luke 12:34 (NIV) — Scripture taken from the Holy Bible, New International Version®, NIV® Copyright ©1973, 1978, 1984, 2011 by Biblica, Inc.® Used by permission. All rights reserved worldwide.

32. Proverbs 21:19 (GNT) — Scripture taken from the Good News Translation in Today's English Version, Second Edition Copyright © 1992 by American Bible Society. Used by Permission.

33. Ecclesiastes 7:2a (NLT) — Scripture taken from the Holy Bible, New Living Translation, copyright © 1996, 2004, 2007 by Tyndale House Foundation. Used by permission of Tyndale House Publishers, Inc., Carol Stream, Illinois 60188. All rights reserved.

34. *Notting Hill.* Written by Richard Curtis. Directed by Roger Michell. Performances by Julia Roberts and Hugh Grant. Universal Pictures, 1999. DVD.

35. Robert B. Sherman and Richard M. Sherman. "A Spoonful of Sugar." 45 RPM. Walt Disney Records, 1964.

36. Ibid.

37. Joel Houston. "Stay and Wait." Zion. CD. Hillsong Music and Sparrow Records, 2013.

Made in the USA
San Bernardino, CA
01 February 2020

63853815R10102